DIARY OF A READY WOMAN

DIARY OF A READY
WOMAN

I Don't Look Like What I've Been Through Because
My Comeback is Better than My Setback

Compiled By: Nekisha Michelle Kee, MSW

Co-Authored By:
Sharice Porter ~ LaVette Cherie ~ Clarissa Foster ~
Angela AJ Thompson
Amber G. ~ L'Divine Holland ~ Kimberly Brown ~
Marla Fowlkes
~ Syrita Lindsey   ~ Sharonda Grandberry
~ Dr. Carla Lindsay ~ LaTonya Spates

Ready WOMAN PUBLISHING

**The Library of Congress Cataloging - in - Publication Data
is available upon request.**

Kee, Nekisha Michelle

Second Edition

ISBN-13: 978-0-9707175-1-1

ISBN-10: 0-9707175-1-2

TABLE OF CONTENTS

WHY THIS BOOK | Letter to the Reader | By Nekisha Michelle

FOREWORD by GregAlan Williams Double Emmy Award-Winner

INTRODUCTION | Dying to be a Ready Woman | By Nekisha Michelle

I will never forget the 21-hour drive from Houston, Texas to Los Angeles, CA. I packed everything I could in my Mercedes Benz S500. My then three-year-old daughter in her car seat was kicking her feet to the Donald Lawrence "Confessions" CD I had on loop...

Diary Entry 1 | The Best is Yet to Come | By Sharice Porter

"Repeat after me: God hates divorce; I will not divorce you," spoke Senior Pastor Jemmings. My soon-to-be husband and I immediately looked at one another and turned around and faced the congregation in disbelief...

Diary Entry 2 | Woman in The Mirror | By LaVette Cherie

As I looked in the mirror I saw nothing, and nothing was familiar to me. I no longer recognized what I saw. The horror story of my life began; my thoughts raced. But truly, it was the beginning of my renaissance...

Diary Entry 3 | Living Past that Moment | By Clarissa Foster

August 11th, 2008 started off like any other day. My alarm clock, which was set only for the weekdays, sounded at precisely 6:30 a.m. Like always, I would grab the remote, tune into the local news to see what was happening in Cleveland...

Diary Entry 4 | The Wealthy Bitch | By Angela AJ Thompson

I wasn't trying to kill myself the day I ran in front of his car. I was just mad and wanted to shake him up, let him know how much he was hurting me. He was the person who, for 15 years, never wanted to see me hurt, but he was tearing my heart out piece by piece...

Diary Entry 5 | Companion of Fools | By Amber G.

Having been forced into a hell, I can attest that I believe he would have killed me if he hadn't dropped his gun. The police were on site escorting me to the ER. My neighbor saved my life; instinct had him swooping that weapon up...

Diary Entry 6 | All Tied Up | By L' Divine Holland

I was pregnant about seven or eight months by Mister, the man I loved and believed loved me. He came to visit, and after not seeing him for the prior three months, we had sex. We role-played, which he loved to do during—at least that's what I thought we were doing. Part of his game was picking me up off the ground by my neck while spilling out demonic chants as he pretended to be Satan...

Diary Entry 7 | And Then I Woke Up | By Kimberly C. Brown

I woke up in my bed crying hysterically, screaming: "My aunt is dead! Oh, my God! Oh, my God!" In my mind, I didn't know if I had already missed the funeral or how many days it had been since she passed. While in grief and thought, I felt a touch on my arm, and a voice from under the sheets said...

Diary Entry 8 | H.U.N.T.E.R. | By Marla Fowlkes

And then she was gone. My baby was dead. Her lifeless body lying in the hospital operating bed—with glassy eyes facing me in a still glare. I was devastated. How could this have happened? How could my 7.2 oz. baby not be alive? My husband Kevin stood there in disbelief with tears in his eyes...

Diary Entry 9 | In My Father's House | By Syrita Lindsey

I awaken in the emergency room, lying in a hospital bed. When I regained my focus, there were a couple of cops in the room appearing to be standing on guard. I scanned the remains of the room and realized that they were perhaps there for me? What the what? Suddenly, I had to pee...

Diary Entry 10| Broken Pieces in a Strong Frame| By Sharonda Grandberry

It was a hot summer day. The humidity was so thick you could hardly breathe. I asked my grandmother if we could go swimming; she said, "yes." I was responsible for ensuring my sister, brother, and cousin arrived at the pool safely. Wiregrass Recreation pool was the place where everyone hangs out, especially the cute boys...

Diary Entry 11 | May I Have Your Attention | By Dr. Carla Lindsay

Rushed to the hospital by my friends, I had taken my college roommate's pills, and nobody knew how many. I was drunk and mad because the guy I liked didn't want anything serious with me. It made me feel invisible. Let's just say, being rushed to the hospital was only the beginning of looking for love in all the wrong places...

Diary Entry 12 | No, Not My Cherry | By LaTonya Spates

I ran to the window and looked out in disbelief... it was gone! The reliable transportation I had for my two children and me! It was my pride. I poured my blood, sweat, and tears into my car. Still, in a tank top and pajama bottoms, I rushed outside to see if it was true. My life was a dreadful nightmare because everything I worked so diligently for was gone...

DIARY OF A READY WOMAN

WHY THIS BOOK

Bouncing back from pitfalls and disasters in my life has been challenging—from being a mother at fourteen to walking out on my first husband in 2009 with a three-year-old. In 2016, I had an epiphany, an Oprah A-ha moment. I wanted to use the power of media and publishing to influence healing, soul growth, and positive thinking in the life of others experiencing difficult and emotional situations. Telling my story wasn't enough; I was hungry to find compelling stories of other women who also passed through pitfalls and personal tragedies. I was looking for women with the gift to turn pain into passion and profits, as I did.

I recruited and interviewed women relentlessly for nearly five months, scouting for women willing to share their story of heartbreak as well as to invest their time and expertise in a book collaboration. Many women came forward, but only those connected to The Ready Woman vision stayed the course.

Through unity, passion, and perseverance, I am proud to present what will be an annual gift to women all over the world for **International Women's Day**: This book, **Diary of a Ready Woman.**

In BLISS,
(Beauty, Love, Intuition, Sensuality, & Significance)

-*Nekisha Michelle*

FOREWORD

A wise man on the south side of Chicago once told me that life's greatest disciplinarians are great suffering and great love; and, so it is with the lives in these pages.Virtually, all of the amazing women in this book have suffered greatly. Often, by the hands and bitter hearts of others and sometimes because they believed, the power of their love and the depth of their commitment, might strengthen the quality of their own questionable choices.

These self-determined "Ready Women" are now ready both because of what they have suffered and in spite of it. Their pain became a kick in the seat of the pants, a tsunami— a giant wave that could either destroy them completely or wash them ashore, battered and bruised but on solid ground.

Tired, defeated, and confused, sheroes who, somehow, mustered the courage to look back at the destruction that was their lives and take honest inventory. Thus, armed with the hard and hurtful truth about themselves and others, these remarkable women began their journeys anew— nurtured and guided by the love of God, love for self, family, and perhaps a true friend.

Failure and heartbreak can mark the beginnings of a powerful new life. Sometimes being lost forces you to finally find your way. The quality of our choices determine the quality of our lives. The choices of African-American women continue to provide foundation and framework not only for their own lives but also for families and communities as well.

I am who I am not only because of my own choices (good and not so good) but because a flawed and foolish young African-American woman took early stock of her own poor choices and recognized the impact those choices might have on her newborn son.

The clarity granted by her willingness to examine and accept full responsibility for the role she had played in her own suffering as well as her decision to no longer suffer fools nor fatally flawed men, led Sister Georgia to commit herself to the daily cultivation of better choices for us both. Her journey from victim to victory was, at first, driven (disciplined) by suffering; the shock, sorrow, and, shame, bourn of betrayal. Then, love became the engine; the love of God, the love she found in her own talents and abilities, and, the love she poured into her son.

Perhaps, all of these insightful authors would agree that, ultimately, "love is the answer." Yet, so many of them, betrayed and heartbroken, chose to abandon love, at least for a time. Many of these stories contain moments when the writer gritted her teeth and suppressed her natural desire for romantic relationship. This kind of sacrifice reminds us that sometimes a sister must be willing to suffer loneliness in order to discover who she really is and the woman she wishes to become.

Flawed and sometimes foolish, blinded by love, duty, and the expectations of others, these wise and wonderful women have gathered their courage and gathered together to share their experience, strength, and hope. You would do well to listen.

Yet, listening is one thing and hearing is quite another. I pray that as you listen to their voices, **The Creator** will, also, bless you with the gift of hearing.

And so it is.

Peace and Blessings

GregAlan Williams
Double Emmy Award-Winner

Facebook: /GregoryAlanWilliams
Twitter: @GregAlanW
Instagram: @GregAlan101
www.GregoryAlanWilliams.com

MEET GREGORY ALAN WILLIAMS

Double Emmy Award-Winning Actor, GregAlan Williams, is widely known for his role (of seven seasons) as beach cop Garner Ellerbee on the most watched television show in the world, Baywatch. He is, most recently, recognized for his portrayal as Robert "Mac" McCready on OWN's hit drama series, Greenleaf.

His 30-year Hollywood career began as a founding member of the world-renowned Penumbra Theater in St. Paul, MN. From there he went on to do stage work with Pulitzer Prize Winner, August Wilson, as well as the Chicago Shakespeare Repertory Theater, Chicago Theater Company, Mixed Blood and Chicago's Goodman Theater.

To date, his broad list of acting credits include recurring roles on the USA Network'sNecessary Roughness, BET'sThe Gameand HBO'sThe Sopranos and his 250 primetime appearances include The West Wing, NCIS: Los Angeles and Castle. His film career boasts 42 feature films, including celebrated classics such as Remember the Titans (Denzel Washington), In the Line of Fire (Clint Eastwood) and Old School (Will Ferrell). Other recent film credits include, Terminator Genysis (Arnold Schwarzenegger), Misconduct (Al Pacino), Hidden Figures (Taraji P. Henson) and more!

GregAlan also the owner and dean of the Actor's Breakthrough film actors training studio in Atlanta.

dear diary

INTRODUCTION

DYING TO BE A READY WOMAN

August 15, 2009

I will never forget the 21-hour drive from Houston, Texas to Los Angeles, CA. I packed everything I could in my Mercedes Benz S500, to include my then three-year-old daughter, in her car seat kicking her feet to the Donald Lawrence "Confessions" CD I had on loop. Here I was, appearing to be successful and having it all. A master's degree, internet radio personality, my own home-based Life Coaching business, married for 5 years, and a mother. I was living in a beautiful townhome overlooking a lake where ducks and fish made their home. But as impressive as it all seemed, MY truth had finally surfaced: These trappings were fillers for my empty soul, my broken heart, and my belief that I was not worthy of happiness and I was not worthy of true love. So, with hot tears running down my cheeks and my heart pounding with fear and anxiety, I LEFT.

I finally got mad and tired enough to let it go and leave it all behind. That life looked good, but was killing my soul, my personality, and my ability to know what made me happy. I was married to an emotional wreck—a man whose character was likened to that of a cobra. He was the type whom everyone loved, and he'd give you the shirt off his back. He worked countless hours to ensure all our bills were paid, and that we had everything we needed. However, I knew him as the ruthless, emotionally abusive tyrant that made me feel like a helpless and hopeless little girl in my own home. I was berated daily for not being good enough. I wasn't a good mother. I was too fat and too lazy. I was cursed at and ignored. He never wanted to go anywhere with me, nor did he invite me to his social gatherings, and he always spoke in his native tongue.

One day, I got out of the house to attend a girlfriend's gathering. My newly ex-husband kept calling my cell phone. I didn't hear the ringing because it was in my purse. When I saw his missed calls, I tried to phone him back only to find that he'd had my cell phone service disconnected. He was punishing me for not being at his beck and call.

I remember countless arguments, during which all he did was insult me by calling me stupid and an idiot. My mind flashes back to the time I was with our daughter at the park. She was about two years old and loved the sliding board. All of the kids were going up the sliding board and jumping from the top. I didn't realize my toddler was entertained by watching the other kids jump off. Before I knew it, she too had climbed to the top of the sliding board, and instead of sliding down, she jumped from the top. So, there I sat, watching my baby drop to the ground filled with dirt and woodchips, from the tallest slide in the park.

She cried a little, but I was super nervous. I called my husband first to tell him what happened and he told me to meet him at home so we could take the baby to the hospital. Feeling sad and afraid I met him at home only to walk into an ambush of insults and belligerent behavior.

He called me a stupid fat bitch, and accused me of allowing his baby to fall. Hollering that he was going to take his baby and get her a new mother, he snatched her from my arms and told me to shut up and get in the car. He cursed and fussed the entire ride to the hospital.

When we arrived at the emergency room, she was examined. The doctor said she was fine and reassured my husband that this is a regular occurrence, that children are curious and will do all kinds of things that put them in harm's way. My future ex-husband just looked at me with that evil smirk and remained quiet. Once he was sure the baby was okay, he took us home, then he went back out to work.

There was no "I am sorry for overreacting" or any other sign of repentance. I'd like to say that was the only blowout, but there were so many that I had begun feeling remorseful for marrying this man. I should tell you, however, that it is my fault. I thought that because I was a plus-sized woman, I'd never have a chance at real love. He was the first man who had ever asked me to marry him, and I said yes. I didn't want to be alone.

Five years was way too long to be in a relationship that wasn't feeding my soul. After a 10-day juice fast, I decided there should be more to my life than being the target of his verbal and mental abuse. It hurt me to my core to leave him for the unknown, but I was dying inside. I was more than a mother and homemaker; there was something inside of me that was sick and tired of feeling like I was the least of all, struggling and reliving the pain of being the target of another person's anger and hostility.

Weary of being suppressed, inhibited, and invisible, I was now ready to break the invisible chains of my life and emerge, unleash, and answer the call ringing deep inside my soul to be free and happy. I was finally READY to live my life by my own rules and on my terms.

THE BOLD EXIT

I packed what I could while he was at work and got on the road to Los Angeles, CA. One thing I know for sure is when you're ready, you don't have to make an announcement, create an argument, or evoke a dramatic exit. You just hold your head high, straighten your back, get what you need, and boldly move into a new life. At least, that is what I did.

I wish I could say this was the only time RUNNING away from a situation was my solution. I had a habit of trying to please people who didn't love me and trying to take care of others while not taking care of myself. Not checking in on my feelings and what I wanted had become a habit.

This time I had to deal with my barriers to my inner confidence and feeling like I never mattered. I decided to take a deep dive into the very essence of my soul—my core being—and uncover all the trauma I tried to bury and forget. I may have looked like I was satisfied and happy, but that was not my truth. I was winging it, trying to do things I thought would make me popular and well-liked, getting high from proving others wrong about what I could and could not do.

Deep down inside, I never felt ready, and I never felt like I deserved any of what I had worked so hard for. It meant nothing and it wasn't satisfying. I had this self-fulfilling prophecy that caused me to believe that as soon as I'd feel a little happiness, it would be all taken away—akin to my foreclosed home, two car repossessions, and bankruptcy. Happiness was so very short-lived, and I didn't like myself because I didn't enjoy my life. That dislike showed up in everything, from lack of money to a lack of genuine love and relationships and the inability to feel like I could fit in.

The more I achieved, the more I lost. I could not build, I found myself rebuilding, restarting, redesigning but not evolving and stabilizing. In fact, one of my life-mentors, Debrena Jackson Gandy, asked me in her deep reflective and stimulating way, "Woman, why are you manifesting great things, and then breaking your magic wand?" I never had an answer. I only knew that this was how it was for me. I would experience greatness and then it would be over, and I'd be back in the pit of just trying to make it.

I noticed my life was going in a ridiculous circle and I wasn't gaining anything; I would stop trying. I'd become afraid to try because I knew eventually some disaster would come and take it all away. When big opportunities came to me, I would shrink and say, I am not ready. I needed to lose weight. I needed to have more education. I needed to have the right mentor. I needed more money. I had an excuse for not leaping when the opportunity came. Later, I would find that someone else took the leap and I'd watch them live the life I wanted for myself. Mad as hell, I would feel rejected by God and life itself, and become engulfed in a fury of envy. I was miserable as hell!

I still hadn't realized I need to deal with the demons in my past, beginning with the emotional pitfalls I endured as a child. They bled into every area of my life, forcing me to repeat the same emotional distress. I am not enough: Rejected, always second-best, the strong gut-wrenching knots in the pit of my stomach reminding me that I was too fat, too short, too loud, too needy, too fast, and too much of a risk. The feelings of fear and torment imparted to me by a well-meaning family that passed on to me, their anxieties and anger about life. Left in a long-time battle of my mind and spirit to entertain situations that reinforced my worthless feelings, I was spent.

I had mixed feelings about what I was good enough to have and who I was good enough for. Those mixed feelings ran my life, the life that I hated living. I was waiting for some miracle, or to be discovered, to be loved thoroughly, to be happy, to have prosperity, to create a movement that mattered, to ask for the sale, to get what I wanted.

I was always waiting for the approval.

THE APPROVAL

I had not recognized that I was my own soul's enemy. I refused to follow my heart due to fear of letting others down, resulting in me being rejected and not being liked. I did not realize that the power to shape my world into the way I wanted to see it has always been inside of me, and always will be.

I thought I needed permission to be okay with myself. My thick thighs, my big butt, my big breasts, my loud mouth, my big hair, my strong intuitive insight and entrepreneurial spirit: These were ALL portions of me. I thought I needed permission to be myself. In retrospect, I wasted time waiting—waiting for approval, waiting for cheerleaders, waiting for the support and encouragement of others.

I finally found out that waiting for permission to be you and embrace your true self will eat away at your soul, your purpose, your reason for being. I finally considered the eyes of my soul and said what I had been waiting for so long to hear from others. What I had been waiting for my parents to say and my family to realize and verbalize was that they were proud of me. I could do anything, and no one could stop or hinder my purpose. The greatest revelation of all was accepting that I am beautiful, lovable, intuitive, sensual, and significant. I am BLISS! Where there is bliss, self-love exists.

When my soul feels good, it's all good. I didn't need permission; I just needed to break my invisible chains. I finally found out that I was the answer to my problems, my unhappiness, and my fears. I had to stop waiting for the world to endorse me and get in the driver's seat of my own life, and start endorsing myself. I understand that many women struggle and fight with their greatness, because we are trying to prove our worth to people who don't even know their own worth.

We end up losing sight of why we started the fight. Within eight months of arriving in Los Angeles, CA, I'd taken $1500 and created the life I'd always dreamed for myself. My ex was shocked that I had the balls to leave his mean ass; he, like many others could not believe I was doing it! I had two great jobs, a part-time business, my cute apartment, and I was on the morning news segment of KTLA as a Relationship Expert. When you step into your READY WOMAN power, you are irresistible, unstoppable, and influential!

Give yourself choices and opportunity to put the oxygen mask on you first before helping anyone else. That oxygen mask is love. Love is oxygen to the soul. If you don't love yourself, no one—and I mean no one—will love you either. You are the leader and CEO of your life. However, you can only lead when you are READY.

Of course, my ex did try everything to save the marriage, but when I decided to move, I moved on. I resolved that I deserved more, and I knew that once I got myself and my life together, he would crave me. And he did. I understood that for us to work, he needed to accept responsibility for his actions and do some work. He wasn't willing, and therefore, I filed for divorce and received my freedom.

I learned how to be a Ready Woman—which is to say, a woman of influence. Now prepare to read the private details—a diary, so to speak—from my companions. You should know that you are going through, and went through, that pain to get ready. I am going to teach you. It's a process of getting ugly and dirty first, but I promise by the end of reading this diary you will never lack anything when you embrace and unleash The Ready Woman inside of you.

DIARY OF A READY WOMAN

The pages of this diary are the paths and personal secret truths of 12 empowered women who experienced very dark periods of the soul, tormented by situations in life that could have killed their desire to live out their unique purpose. Instead of giving up, each took responsibility for their trauma and found resolve, acceptance, and divine strength to rise and unleash the superwoman power within and become unstoppable in their faith in God and their faith in themselves to succeed.

This diary is the recounting of situations that, although heart-wrenching, will leave you feeling speechless and determined to overcome the dark period of your life, and turn that pain into a platform of influence and income. This diary is learning from the inside out, to become a courageously authentic woman. A Ready Woman!

A Ready Woman overcomes her worst life challenges; she's fine with being vulnerable; she knows what did not kill her made her READY to win. She is a champion in every area of her life. A Ready Woman knows what she is made of, and that her experiences, her voice, her expertise and even her pain MATTERS.

When you're a READY WOMAN, you learn to break your invisible chains and do what the 12 ladies and I are discussing.

1. Take charge of your soul and your story.
2. Turn each painful lesson into something beautiful and lasting.
3. Help others like you find their way to the light and brilliance inside.

A Ready Woman creates a new paradigm for her life with the belief that she is worthy of anything she wants. She can have love and live happily. All she must do is snatch her power back.

THE READY WOMAN MANTRA...

I now accept and receive: It takes God, Grit, & Bliss to turn my challenges and problems into a platform for love, income, & influence. Although I come as one, I stand as many because I am the Ready Woman.

The OATH

I can, and I will, live as a woman of income and influence, because all the hell I've lived through was only to put me on the path toward **THE READY WOMAN**. I accept the blessings and own the behavior and Bliss of the Ready Woman. I Am the Ready Woman today and always!

I am signing below for confirmation—that I Am the Ready Woman—and accept all lessons, rights, and blessings because of taking control of my soul and my life. As I read this sacred diary, I will incorporate the lessons immediately into my life, so that I can experience my paradigm shift and welcome more happiness, love, income, and influence without doubt or disbelief.

Signature: _____

Date: _____

MEET THE VISIONARY, NEKISHA MICHELLE

The world's most beloved Love Doyenne, Matchmaker, and owner of a lifestyle and personal improvement brand—Ready Woman Experience—as well as the founder of Ultimate Match Agency—a dating agency providing boutique matchmaking services and events for the bold, intentional, and upscale professional. She's been featured in everything from Ebony, Black Enterprise, Upscale, Rolling Out, Success, and Plus Model Magazine, to being a TV Personality on OWN and HGTV.

Nekisha Michelle redesigned her life after being a social worker and working in non-profit administration for over 16 years to share her story and passion of finding real love for herself as a plus-size woman using BLISS. She believes everyone can be happy and have amazing love. "Understanding it is not about a shape or size, but having the right state of mind."

Nekisha is a lady of Alpha Kappa Alpha Sorority, Inc., and received her bachelor degree from Virginia State University (HBCU) and a Masters of Social Work in 1999 from the University of Cincinnati.

She is the wife to Boyo and mother of Ciera "Ce Ce" and Islamyaat "Izzy."

Nekisha Michelle carries a powerful inspiring voice, engaging personality, and passion for helping others create an amazing life through speaking, coaching, live training, and events.

Nekisha is the author of The Ready Woman, How to Bounce Back from Adversity, and Redesign Your Life for Amazing Love and Real Happiness.

www.ultimatematchagency.co
www.instagram.com/thereadywoman/
www.youtube.com/nekishamichelle
Support@nekisha-michelle.com

Diary Entry 1
The Best is Yet to Come
By Sharice Porter

dear diary

God Hates Divorce

"Repeat after me: God hates divorce; I will not divorce you," spoke Senior Pastor Jemmings. My soon-to-be husband and I immediately looked at one another and turned around and faced the congregation in disbelief. These were not the words we wrote in our marriage vows. Nonetheless, we chuckled and repeated after him. I should have paid attention because those words were a sign from above. I ignored the sign and many other signs.

One year later I was signing divorce papers. My husband decided that the woman who so eloquently sang 'The Best is Yet to Come' by Donald Lawrence at our wedding was a better companion for him than I was.

Every little girl dreams of the day she will meet her knight in shining armor and be whisked off to live happily ever after. I had suppressed those thoughts after a dark period in my life. In 1999, I lost my mom to a heart attack. I had already lost my older brother three years earlier from complications of kidney failure. I tried to come out from the dark cloud that was over me when in 2002 my sister-in-law was killed by a drunk driver.

My niece had already lost her father, and the thought of her becoming an orphan in that way sent me into a downward spiral. A week after I got back home from my sister in law's funeral in Southern California I still wasn't ready to go back to work. I stayed in bed all day. I didn't want to eat. I was depressed.

I was heartbroken. I felt like I left my niece Nikki behind even though she was staying with her mother's side of the family. I didn't know what that meant for seeing her again. I was afraid and feeling hopeless. I wanted her with me. I didn't have children of my own, so she was everything to me.

I had many thoughts of suicide, I felt like leaving this life and going to be with my deceased family members that left me behind. It got so dark that I drove myself to the hospital and told the doctor on call about what I was feeling. The doctor set me up with a psychiatrist and advised me to go home and rest. I decided that I would drown my sorrows in alcohol and parties.

My dear friend Sharon called me to go out on a Friday night, and I jumped at the chance to get away from my thoughts for a moment. I was on my way out the door when Crystal another friend called and asked me to come with her to bible study. Partying or bible study were my choices. The choice was not a hard one to make but for some reason when I told my friend about the change in plans she said we can do both.

I enjoyed the sermon, and I felt comfortable at this church. There was a young group of people there that Friday night. I thought that was very interesting and I decided I would go back to Sunday service one day. I was in the lobby talking with my friend Crystal that invited me, and she advised that the next day there was a singles conference there and she pleaded for me to go.

Living Single

Crystal said the cost was $40. I had just gotten back to work, and I had used up all my sick time and excused absences, as well as, unpaid days. I didn't have the money to spend. I was advising her of this fact, and just as I had stated this a young lady said just come tomorrow, and your name tag will be waiting for you. I couldn't believe it. I asked her if she was sure and she said yes, be here tomorrow.

The next morning, I was there at church, bright and early and just as she stated I had a name tag. I learned a lot during the general session. I was feeling lighter like that heavy weight that I had been carrying was being lifted. It was time to go to the breakout sessions, and the choices were how to be a good single parent and how to manage your finances. I didn't need to learn about being a single parent, so I went to the finance class.

After the class was over it was lunchtime. Crystal couldn't stay to eat lunch, so I was left alone to get through the rest of the day. I was standing in line for lunch, and I overheard a group of people in front of me mention the name of a person that I knew. I decided to introduce myself to them and tell them that I knew Shawn also. There were two girls and one guy.

Once I got my food, I followed my new group of associates to a table and sat down and chatted with them. We had a pleasant conversation. The man Dimitri caught my attention and was very charming and pleasant to the eyes. When the singles in attendance came back together in the final general session, Dimitri was sitting several rows behind me. After the session was over, he came up to me and said,

"I don't know, I don't think I can live up to the church's expectations of how singles are supposed to live. Do you want to exchange information and help each other?"

Dimitri and I exchanged information, and he called my cell phone while I was on my way home from the conference. We had a pleasant conversation and said we would see one another the next morning at church. He was two years younger than me. He worked in Information Technology and he grew up in the church. The conversation was easy, and I immediately felt comfortable with him.

The next morning, I got to church early. I found my seat in the front and took the next seat as well and filled it up with my books and my purse. I looked up towards the front door, and there he was. The day before Dimitri wore a pair of jeans and a corduroy jacket with a hat, but on Sunday he was dressed in a blue suit that fit him perfectly.

He was chatting with someone at the door. I looked away and giggled to myself and said *"my, my, my."* Just then I heard him say

"Is that seat taken?"

I said, *"oh no"* as I threw my belongings to the floor.

He sat next to me, and when the altar call came, we both went up to join the church. My eyes were closed, so I didn't see him come up but once we were told to go back to sign up I opened my eyes, and he was right there.

We were inseparable. We spent every day together. We went to bible study and all of the other church activities together. I was falling. I just knew God had sent me an angel. After all the turmoil that I had been through my broken heart was on the mend.

My pastor introduced a new class for singles called 'Preparing for Marriage.' We signed up and received our 'Preparing for Marriage' books. Dimitri and I read the book and completed our pre-wedding assignments. We were instructed that once we got to page 152 of the book, we had a decision to make. That was the moment that we were supposed to acknowledge any red flags and decide to stay together or dismantle the relationship.

He Proposed

One evening about six months later, Dimitri, the man I met while at the singles conference, invited me to his house. I was in his restroom when Dimitri started screaming my name like the house was on fire! I ran to see why he was hollering my name, there he was with candles lit, soft music playing. He was on one knee. I couldn't believe it! I looked at the candles, there was a shiny object in the middle.

"Will you make me a happy man? Will you marry me?"

Of course, I said yes. We began planning our wedding immediately. I was happy. My family was happy, and so was his.

Cold Feet

As we got closer to the wedding, I started to get cold feet. We put the cart before the horse and bought a house before we were married. We moved in six months before the wedding. Once our pastor found out, he told Dimitri to leave.

Dimitri moved out for a moment, but he didn't feel it was necessary to pay a mortgage on a house and live elsewhere. Several weeks before the wedding I went through a period of doubt, the church had gotten to me. I felt that we were living in sin. I didn't want to disobey God. I didn't know much about religion at the time since I was a "babe in Christ". I took a couple of days off from work. I would lie in my bed and cry all day. I called his mom.

"I want to call the wedding off."

"You just have wedding jitters. You're going to be a beautiful bride and everything will be okay." She assured me. I got myself together and decided to go forward with the wedding.

Our wedding was amazing. People would see us months after and say:

"Your wedding was the bomb!" Others would say,
"Your wedding was the best wedding I have ever been too."

We were happy to know everyone had a good time. The honeymoon was great too. We went on a cruise to the Western Caribbean.

At the Beginning of the Marriage

The first six months, things were good. I remember when my amazing husband helped me take the braids out of my hair. Dimitri was the perfect gentleman. He was very attentive. I wanted for nothing. Friday nights were date nights. I had a hard time keeping the smile off my face. We had fun together. He was spontaneous. He would start driving, and we would end up in Disneyland or Reno.

Then what seemed like all of a sudden about month seven the whispers from various church members started about our marriage. I got a warning that my husband was seen out with a girl in the choir at a restaurant.

We were both members of the choir at church. I sang alto, and he sang tenor. Church choir members thought it was so cute to see us singing in the choir. I enjoyed singing in church. We even sang at a Fred Hammond concert. I didn't know it at the time but my singing days were just about over.

I had other aspirations at church. I wanted to become an usher. My husband knew this. He started asking me about it and said I should leave the choir and start my ministry as an usher. I thought he was trying to help me with my Christian walk. I thought he only wanted me to walk in my gift. I had no clue at the time what the real reason was that he no longer wanted me to be a part of the choir.

I stopped going to choir rehearsal on Tuesday nights and began meeting with the usher board on Saturdays. Shortly after my transition, I noticed my husband started coming home late from choir rehearsal. I also noticed that he had begun talking to another choir member on the phone named Stacy. I didn't think much of it until he mentioned that he would like to help this woman with the purchase of a home. Even with that proposal, I figured he was just thinking about our financial future. I had no reason to believe that there was anything else going on.

One evening he came home late from choir rehearsal. I was already in bed. He walked into the house with the phone to his ear. He was having an in-depth conversation with someone. He walked into the bedroom kissed me on my forehead and said Stacy needed some advice from a man. Dimitri stated he would finish his conversation and be in the bedroom later. I was a little upset at the fact that he didn't end his conversation when he walked through the door, but again I had no reason at the time to think anything of the conversation.

An Ugly Pattern Started

I won't say I was naïve, but I still didn't think much of people saying they saw my husband out with Stacy because we were all friends. We were in the choir together. I didn't believe that it was wrong of them to eat together.

On our one-year anniversary, he had to put our celebration on hold to be a part of choir rehearsal with another choir. I was distraught. We walked into the rehearsal, and there Stacy was. I was feeling very agitated about the laughing and joking that they were doing, but I just sat back and watched.

He did take me to dinner for our anniversary, but once we got home, he asked me how I felt about us and where we were in our marriage. I said it was our first year, I knew there would be bumps along the way, but with time it would become smooth. He just listened.

"So, you think we are good?" he questioned.

"I know we are not good, but everyone says the first year is rough. We're just getting to know one another." I wasn't worried.

"I don't know man. I just don't know," he replied. I didn't know what to think about his answer, but I knew I believed that God had put us together and He would keep us together.

Several months after our anniversary a couple of married couples that we were close to were having a get together on the 4th of July. We said that we were going to go to the event months prior. Now we were in a weird space, but we had already RSVP'd for the event so we couldn't back out.

Set Up for Failure

I was having trouble with my job. I had been working for the same company for over four years. I worked in every department of my employment. My boss noted she was 'grooming me for management.' Yeah, right. She was setting me up for failure.

One morning I was working in the front taking money for payments when our computers went down. All of the management had just left the office to get their morning coffee. All of the cashiers had to start writing paper tickets for receipts.

Why did I have to get an angry customer with a lot of cash who wanted a regular receipt? I told the customer that our computers were down. I wrote her information on a separate paper giving her a copy. I wrapped the cash the customer gave me in a rubber band with the hand-written receipt on top.

There was a long line for the membership department so there was no way I could stop and go lock up the money. I continued to take payments until my boss asked me to complete another task. I knew that I had to explain the money to the next cashier, but I figured I would do that at the end of the day.

At the end of the day my drawer came up short, and the customer's payment did not get posted. I didn't have a clue as to what happened to that money, but because I took the cash, I was held responsible.

The next couple of days I searched every payment in the system for an overpayment. I searched my drawer. I asked around to see if anybody knew what happened to the money. I am a child of God I don't steal. I especially would not take from my job. I had been talking to my friend Nita about my situation through job email. Nita told me she had to hide some shoes that she bought from her husband. She mentioned the shoes cost a lot of money and he wouldn't like that she spent so much. I had no clue that this email would become evidence in the case against me in losing my job.

My supervisor put me on administrative leave with pay. My marriage got worse than before. I thought for sure that they would find the money and I would be told to come back to work. I was off from work for one week. I went back in for an interview with Human Resources. I was released from my job permanently.

I had never been fired from a job before. I knew what I had done, and I knew what I had not done. I tried to plead my case, but there was no one to hear me. The decision was final. The email about the shoes backfired, and it appeared that I had gone shopping and bought expensive shoes with the money that I took from my job.

In the beginning, my husband was supportive he helped me with my resume and sent me job listings. Then it was like Dr. Jekyll and Mr. Hyde. The next thing I knew he decided to sell our house. He told me that it would be better if we moved closer to family and his job, while we sorted things out and I found a new job. I was only out of work for several weeks, but it was several weeks too late. During this time, everything fell apart.

I was at church one day minding my own business, and my husband decided to go off on me outside of the church. One of the church members saw me with tears in my eyes, and she took me outside to talk. I told her what was going on. I told her my marriage was over. Marilyn said we would work it out, it was still new and that we would get through it. I knew it wasn't that simple, but I could never imagine what would happen next.

After church, I was getting ready to leave, and one of the Minister's wives came up to me and said she wanted me to come to her house for dinner. Angela said it was imperative that I go with her after church. She said she needed to talk to me. I followed her to her house and she made dinner.

She told me the sordid details of what I feared the most. Angela said that her friend Stacy and my husband had been having an affair for months. She said she should have told me months ago. Angela went to Stacy and advised her to stop in the beginning, but she didn't see any change. Angela's husband John came home and suggested that he was putting in a call to Dimitri. I heard John raise his voice quoting scripture to Dimitri. He hung up the phone and came into the room where we were sitting.

"Well, your husband says he's finished with the marriage. He says he can't do this with you anymore." My heart sank. Angela and John urged me to call my pastor and tell him what was going on. I called the pastor, and he called my husband. I still had to go home. We slept in separate rooms that night.

Stacy can Have Him

After everything that I had been through I just knew that GOD had sent me an angel that would take care of my already fragile heart. Instead, it was as if the devil himself had decided to take what was left of my fragile heart and tear it into a million pieces. I reached out to Stacy and asked her point blank if she wanted my husband. She tried to make it seem like they were just friends.

"No, I don't want your husband," she replied.

"You can have him you just need to be woman enough and come clean about the relationship."

She continued to stick to her story that they were just friends. It was depressing to be in the house day after day looking at the rooms that I thought I would fill with children. I was there when Realtors came by with prospective buyers. I was boiling when the house sold, and the new owners came by to check out the things that they wanted us to fix before they moved in.

Where was I going to go now? How could I tell my family that all of the hard work they put into my wedding was for nothing?

My family welcomed me back with open arms. I moved in with my grandmother and waited for the divorce to be final. Four months after the ink dried on our divorce papers he married Stacy in Las Vegas. I didn't think my heart could take it...but GOD.

Slowly but surely, I started going back to church. I worked hard to stand firm even when the looks and the whispers made me want to run. I continued my duties as an usher for another year before I decided to find a new church home. Although it was one of the hardest times in my life, I persevered. I moved on with my life.

THE READY WOMAN

I sold black art and traveled to many exotic spots. I wrote my first book and started speaking. I started an organization for young girls called *'InPowerment University.'* The tagline is "Helping young women look inside themselves to ignite the power within so they can shine in their own lives."

Diary of a Ready Woman

I purchased a new home, on my own. I had to learn to shine in my own life despite the things I went through. I have finally realized through it all that the things that happened to me, happened for me, because a ready woman needs to know her power. I now know that when disappointments come, I can handle it. I will not break down and die. Every problem has an expiration date. What is for me, is for me and no one can take that away.

So, to you ready woman, I want you to realize that although you will go through things in life, it will never keep you from what you are supposed to have and where you are meant to be.

When you are in the middle of your challenge I want you to find your power, get excited because there is an expiration date and what's next is nothing short of amazing. Trust God. Trust yourself and trust the process.

Yes, Stacy was right, The Best is Yet to Come!

About the Author

Sharice Porter is the visionary and co-founder of INPowerment University where the goal is to help young girls search within themselves to find the power that already lives within each of them.

As a child, Sharice faced many hardships the first of which changed the trajectory of her life. Her mother had a stroke when Sharice, was just nine years old. The shock of her mother's illness changed her from a happy child into a girl with no hope. The struggles of her home life often kept her feeling like she was all alone. The pain and turmoil she experienced from childhood to adulthood hardened her heart. She dreamed of a better life for herself.

She is the first in her immediate family to graduate from college. She obtained her Bachelor's Degree in Mass Communications from Cal State University, Hayward. While in school she wrote for the campus newspaper, *"The Pioneer"*, and had aspirations of becoming a published author and speaker. Those hopes were realized in July of 2016 when she became a featured author in the book compilation *"Breaking Through Barriers."*

She accepted Jesus Christ as her Lord and Savior, and HE began to show her the reasons behind the heartache and pain she experienced in her childhood. She took a life changing solo trip to Hawaii in 2013 where she discovered her passion and began developing what would later become 'INPowerment University.'

Diary of a Ready Woman

With her message of faith and determination, she hopes to reach young girls and women that may feel hurt by what life has thrown at them. She wants to show them that even though they may have had rainy days in their past a rainbow is always on the other side. She has come a long way by faith, and she realizes because of her belief in GOD all things are possible to obtain.

Through her books and motivational speaking, her mission is to inspire and empower girls and women to understand that even though there may be some scars in life with time scars do heal.

psharice@hotmail.com
www.facebook.com/sharice.porter
www.instagram.com/shortbody72/

Dedication and Acknowledgements

This chapter is to the women that take a chance on "love." Your heart may get broken just remember that you are beautiful, strong and you have everything inside of you to make your dreams come true.

I would like to acknowledge Tanicia "Shamay Speaks" Currie for helping me make one of my dreams come true. Thank you for assisting me with telling my story and becoming a published author for the first time in the book compilation *"Breaking Through Barriers."*

Personal Notes:

_____

_____

_____

_____

_____

_____

_____

_____

_____

_____

_____

Diary Entry 2
Woman in The Mirror
By LaVette Cherie

dear diary

It's me LaVette...   *November 18, 2000*

The Blow Was Powerful

As I looked in the mirror I saw nothing, and nothing was familiar to me. I no longer recognized what I saw. The horror story of my life began; my thoughts raced. But truly, it was the beginning of my renaissance.

Vernon was finally making his way to the car, and as I watched him walk towards me, I realized that I would no longer keep my mouth shut. He got inside the car and immediately dropped profanities, especially the infamous word:

"Bitch!" He yelled.
"You're a liar and a cheater I don't deserve this abuse!" I screamed back quickly.

"You always ruin everything. You're a crazy bitch, and our marriage is over." Vernon became explosive.

"You have never been honest with me, and I know you cheated and had an affair." I blurted out.

"No, you're insecure and jealous." He responded.

"I found the card." I said smugly. In the next second, I saw a fisted hand coming at my face.

The blow was powerful, and I felt as if I was going to pass out. But with all my strength, I held on. I immediately looked at my eye in the mirror, weeping hysterically.

"My father is going to kill you." I began beating him and tearing his shirt. The car was veering into other lanes, but in this pain, I was ready to die. I did not know how I was going to face this tragedy in my life. In a split second, everything had changed. It's over, I thought; how was I going to move on? How are my daughters and family going to feel? I knew that I needed to get the strength to end this toxic marriage from somewhere.

I'll start from the beginning...

It was a cloudy, rainy day, as I sat there in the limo with the girls and their father, my first husband, AJ, Sissy, and dad in front of the church. My brother couldn't make it as he was stuck out at sea, I hated he couldn't be with us today. Vernon walked by and AJ called out his name. Everyone said, *"who is Vernon?"*

"This was the worst day of my life." Little did I know that it wasn't because of the death of my mother, but it was because of the connection with Vernon, and this became a hell that attempted to crush my soul. So, as the sun fell, my story, of an abusive relationship began!

Fiery Red Hair Caught my Attention

It was a Saturday night, and we were headed to New York to let go and have fun. My cousin wanted to introduce us to his fraternity brothers.

"Ok geez can we just go inside?" I questioned.

"No, I have someone I 'd like you to meet," Adam said.

So, we headed to the restaurant next to the club and there he was. My eyes saw a man wearing well-polished Gators, and they mesmerized me.

I looked up his smile and fiery red hair caught my attention, and that turned me on.

Vernon was just promoted to rank as an officer, in the United States Navy and he also held a prestigious position at a lending institution. I go for the 'Al B Sure' type by looks with an entrepreneur spirit. Vernon was the Morris Chestnut type, very professional gangster with an education.

A few months passed since I met Vernon and we hardly ever communicated. I thought of him but was in the middle of a divorce and wasn't ready to make any commitments. The first time I saw him after the day we met, he was passing by the limo just before my mother's funeral. The saddest day of my life and all I could see was black.

As time passed Vernon and I talked more and started dating. We enjoyed jazz, fine dining, traveling, and after dating for a year, we decided that neither could live without the other. Six months after our engagement he was deployed.

During this deployment was the beginning of where lies, trust, and scandal began. Vernon would act strange, not reachable, always out of town, and I started to suspect he was lying to me. He came home for the holidays, you see I could not freely go and visit him, my life revolved around my two daughters, and they always came first.

I knew Vernon was lonely across the states in California, but I had to carry on in Long Island. Once he returned I started noticing the signs of cheating, it all became visible, but I acted as if I didn't see it.

I figured he had been a bachelor for so long it would take a while for him to acclimate to the thought of being a married man. So, as we got through the dating and courting we decided on a commitment of marriage, and this would wrap us all together. I finally introduced Vernon to my family and my precious daughters. They loved him, and he loved them, and I got to meet his son. As time went on, I did notice warning signs, but I ignored them because of what he said.

I value words as words are everything to me. The girl's father stopped paying child support, I lost my job, and I was scared. I had a mortgage, car payment, two kids, and I was struggling. I was absent mostly wondering why God had given me this life. Feeling lost, I grabbed onto Vernon, he assured me not to worry and that he would be there for me. I fell deeper and deeper in love with him and was grateful that he was there.

I'm Married Now

Eventually, we were married, and immediately after marriage, the red flags became excessive. Vernon and I could never communicate about anything, bills, money, cleaning, him keeping late hours at work. Whenever I tried to talk, he would become extremely verbally abusive. I was sick to my stomach trying to make things work out, but I knew deep down it just wasn't.

I went to church and prayed every day that God would bless my marriage. I exercised and took excellent care of myself, and I always cooked and kept a clean home. Many salon visits, hair, nails, and waxing. I just wanted to make him happy, and I wanted his approval.

As time went by the marriage became more and more tumultuous. I wanted to hold on for stability, security, and for my children's well-being. I didn't want them to have too many changes in their lives.

We had so much fun. Great vacations, holidays, and family trips. He showered me with the best gifts, and our sex life was fantastic! This was my reward for all the wrong, abusive things he did to me. I still felt so alone, and that's the worst to be married but feel alone.

He controlled everything I started to realize I was his trophy wife, his jewelry; I was only part of an image. He continued to lie, cheat and became more and more abusive. I still hung onto hope, and since this was my second marriage, it had to work.

Despite everything I put into the marriage it was apparent that as each day passed, I was falling apart. All the deception, secrecy, and cheating just became endless. Vernon had several women. He had an incredible appetite for sex, all kinds, and was very greedy. I decided to investigate my fears. I had woman's intuition, but I wanted to see my pain, I felt that maybe if I can visually see it, I would know, without any doubts, of his cheating lifestyle.

What I Discovered Was Sickening

I installed spyware on our home computer, and I thought maybe I was overreacting, at the same time dreading what would come to light. Astonishing, What I discovered was sickening. I found out he was in communication with many women daily. They would hold long exchanges of emails, talking about their daily routines, vacations, concerts, and sex. He was sending them money, receiving pornographic photos, and planning rendezvous with women I had never met.

After many years of a stormy marriage, it finally arrived on the day of its tragic end. This day was Thanksgiving eve, and I was so excited as Vernon, and I planned to attend a very classy sophisticated event. We decided to have dinner at home instead of going out, and I did not eat much, as I did not want to look fat in my dress. I had the perfect blue dress with cut out on the waist that was very revealing. I felt as if I were a sex kitten in this dress! As I stood in front of the mirror what I saw was an incredible beauty! I hadn't felt this good in a long while and was ready to enjoy all the festivities.

Only I had a strange feeling that night, as I felt upset about something but I just couldn't put my finger on it. So, we head out to the party, I looked at him, he was dapper in his tux, and I was breathtaking. I must admit a charming couple that would attract many eyes and yet I still felt uneasy. You see I felt so small, but when I knew I could draw eyes, this would lift me up.

We arrived, I was very buzzed from drinking my famous Bombay Gin martinis so I really didn't need too much else to drink. As we entered he gave me his car keys and we were immediately greeted by several women who seemed to know him. I felt uneasy about all the lookers, and I asked Vernon if he knew anyone at the party, he replied, "maybe a few of my frat brothers are here, but no I don't know anyone else."

As we walked around, my head turning and seeing eyes rolling, it was very clear he was well known. We preceded to try the wine tasting, and he started flirting right in front of me. I was humiliated and confused but I shrugged it off. We decided to go inside and find a place to sit and possibly try the hors d'oeuvres and dance.

We ended up going to the top level and I must admit it was such an exquisite party with beautiful people. I started to really enjoy myself taking pictures and networking. It was a very special evening and I wanted to take it all in. A lady walked over and hugged him and he introduced me but I was taken by surprise. This woman was the president of the organization and he finally admitted that he did know her and that they have been working on putting together networking events. I understood but I felt betrayed because he's a busy body always keeping in contact with many women. I wasn't jealous I just felt betrayed, Vernon should be my best friend and he should share things with me.

I was more disappointed than anything, suddenly he said it's time to go. I said no I don't want to go and he said we must go! You are drunk and you're not even speaking right. I said no I am fine. Why don't you get me some water or food? Vernon was adamant about leaving and he left me standing there. I stood there and decided to walk downstairs to the dance floor and I realized I had more than my share of alcohol. I became angry and I could not find Vernon. I stood in front of the dance floor for a bit and decided to go outside and look for him.

It was at this moment I realized that I had the car keys and a big smile on my face. I went to the car to wait for him as I sat there every bad memory, every hurt, and every pain that he ever caused me began to fill my thoughts. I could no longer mask this heartache, it was becoming stronger and stronger. All the pain was ready to escape from my mind, body, and soul. I could no longer control it, at this moment, I started looking for things in the car, proof of a cheater because he was a bad liar and I often found receipts, cards, and women's phone numbers. I was so upset as I opened the trunk I found a card from a woman he had an affair with. My heart ached as I could not believe how he just left this kind of proof in our car. I threw everything out of the glove compartment and tears fell from my eyes.

The Black Eye Cover Up

I never reported the incident, in fact, I spent the next 2 months in emotional and physical turmoil. I sacrificed myself for the sake of this marriage and I went on as if nothing happened. I purchased a brand of tattoo makeup to cover my eye and carried on and hid all the pain inside. At work during my proposals or whenever I would be talking to anyone all I could think about was my black-eye. As my colleagues or anyone approached me, all I could think is, can they see my black eye.

I heard voices in my mind, I started to be disgusted with myself. What was even more emotionally damaging is that Vernon would make jokes from time to time about women being beat or talking back. He even insinuated that he never meant to hit me and that I ran into his fist. There was another time after church, we disagreed, and his body language looked as if he wanted to hit me again! I knew deep inside I had to get him out of my life I just didn't know how.

As we celebrated New Year's I didn't feel pretty, in fact, I felt like a loser, as if I betrayed myself. I was lost and mentally checked out. My sales at work dropped tremendously and I was literally functioning as if I were a zombie.

The morning after New Year's I looked in the mirror covering up my eye and when I looked I no longer saw myself. It had just hit me that I was gone, the woman I knew was dead, and this person was not me. I had been gone for a long time, in fact, a decade, the beginning of my relationship with a narcissistic monster! As I leaned into the mirror, I could not look, and there in my glance, I knew that I was in some serious mental trouble. 45 days had passed since being physically assaulted and it was Monday morning. Back to work and was trying to psyche myself up as I had a big proposal. I always got my deals signed.

I Was as the Closer

This day after my proposal did not go well I sat in my car breaking down. Tears pouring down my face, in disbelief, that I had loved another more than I loved myself, I loved an abusive monster. I realized that I could no longer see myself spiraling down, and this black eye was ever so dark on my very light ivory face. I had dug myself into a very dark hole.

I no longer wanted to live and I cried out to God! Lord I do not want to live any longer and I do not understand where I am. I know this is not the life you have for me but I do not know how to get on my path. Lord take my life! I pleaded crying hysterically in my car begging God. I give you my life. Lord please dissipate everything out of my life that's not meant and help me to move forward. Lord, I am not capable of making any decisions in my marriage, career, or for my personal well-being. Take my life Lord I am yours.

From that day on my life had what you call the domino effect. God moved in and moved out all the abuse from my life. Vernon was immediately faded out of my life and I was alone left to grow beyond my own understanding.

I became a new woman, now I saw the light, now I am whole. God created miracle after miracle in my life. Events that I never imagined, my dreams were coming true. I was finally living and all I can say is look at God. I am grateful for this night of tragedy as it left me to discover myself, to find my true purpose of existence.

Today I am living my dream; I have received another chance to create a life filled with love!

THE READY WOMAN

I was beaten severely in my previous relationship, I survived. A refreshing awakening daunted over my family and me. I am living a new life filled with self-love, self-respect, and I am no longer a confused woman. I have several projects I am currently working on as a writer, poet, elocutionist, and public speaker. I am working on marketing and sharing my experiences in hopes to touch all people from all walks of life. I desire to be that inspiration, that guiding light, to help someone realize that it's ok to love yourself.

Abuse in any form should never be tolerated from anyone. It can cause years of pain that can have an everlasting effect. Always look fear in the face and I guarantee your miracles will appear. I would like to say that it's best to listen to your gut. Although I revealed, I am grateful for my experiences I am certain this is not the way God would have wanted me to find my purpose in life. There were many warning signs, and I never listened to my gut as I wanted that marriage more than myself. Forgiveness is another important aspect and very freeing, I have forgiven Vernon, and today I remain cordial.

I now know that every moment you live, you die; so each moment live it to the fullest. It is ok to be selfish, as self-preservation is critical. What I am about to say may sound like a cliché but do it anyway, "Trust in God" and fall in love with the woman in the mirror.

About the Author

LaVette Cherie was born in Sidney Ohio. As a young girl, her mother relocated her to San Bernardino, California, due to a failed marriage of domestic violence. After arriving in California, her mother faced more abuse from a close relative and fled in fear to Long Beach, Ca. Long Beach, is where LaVette embraced her adolescence; this was the 80's era where music, art, and fashion inspired her. Although there were many Rap artist around her, she was attracted to Punk Rock music; she spent a lot of time in the scene clubs.

LaVette later relocated to Seattle Washington, to attend college, after several years there, she moved back to California and started her own family and led a career as a mortgage broker. After raising her children, she experienced a renaissance out of her personal domestic violence experience, which put her on a new life path and calling.

Today, residing in Southern California LaVette Cherie is a Poet, Actress, Writer, and Elocutionist. LaVette Cherie has poetry published in Z Publishing's," and California's Best Emerging Poets." LaVette has work appearing or forthcoming in several theatre venues, including her poems recently featured in a Nina Child's Production play "Scenes From The Bridge". She also appears in local venues to spread love through her poetry, has written lyrics for several artists, working on her first album, and building her elocution business.

LaVette's style is very eclectic as she is cultured and loves reaching all people around the world. If she isn't writing, you can find her traveling, enjoying nature, family, and meditation.

LaVette has a big heart and firmly believes in serving others, she is very giving of herself to her community and country. The United States Army recognized LaVette Cherie for her volunteer contribution. LaVette loves laughter and she lives to surround herself in beauty.

You can visit her at

www.lavettecherie.com
www.facebook.com/lavettecherie
https://www.instagram.com/lavettecherie

Dedication and Acknowledgements

I dedicate this book to my amazing MOTHER who taught me how to live, love, and laugh ... REST in heaven Yolande McMiller, my Aunt Janet, and to my two amazing daughters who went through this journey with me, as I know when I laughed you both laughed when I cried you both cried, and when I began to live so did you! I love you, and I am most grateful for you and your support!

I would like to thank God for shifting my life and placing me on the divine path that designed for me. Second, Nasira God connected us, and we knew we would work together on a project but didn't know it would birth the seed of such a profound and phenomenal book! I thank you for all your advice, wisdom, and partnership! Finally, to the TEAM, this all came together because you had the courage to SHARE! Keep Shining Lovelies.

Personal Notes:

_____

_____

_____

_____

_____

_____

_____

_____

Diary Entry 3
Living Past that Moment
By Clarissa Foster

dear diary

It's me Clarissa...   *January 4, 2007*

"Being Challenged in Life is Inevitable; Being Defeated is Optional."

No Ordinary Day

August 11th, 2008 started off like any other day. My alarm clock, which was set only for the weekdays, sounded at precisely 6:30 a.m. Like always, I would grab the remote and tune into the local news to see what was happening in Cleveland. Then at seven o'clock, I tuned in to watch or listen to the Today Show. I would finally get up, stretch, and head to my bathroom. Lastly, I would proceed to the bedroom next door to wake my son.

That was a chore because he was never eagerly excited about school unless there was an extracurricular activity taking place that day. As he lollygags for the next twenty or so minutes, I was able to think. It was no ordinary day. I did not sleep at all, managing out of pure exhaustion to finally fall asleep around 3:30 a.m. The realization was that today was that fateful day I was to report to Courtroom 17B for my sentencing. "How could they find me guilty?" The case centered around a mortgage broker, not my title company. "Did they understand what was happening? I did my job! Now I'm going to prison!"

Shattered!!! My whole existence had shattered into a million pieces. I was no longer a mother. I was no longer a business owner. I was no longer a daughter. I was no longer free. I was inmate number WO73139. I was dead. At least that is what I felt. Nothing in the world could describe the day I lost my freedom. It was like an out-of-body experience.

THE EARLY YEARS

"Focus on Mastery"
– by #IamMirrorMessages

As a child, my dreams were astronomical. I wanted to be an astronaut. I wanted to be the first black female astronaut. I was taught early on about trailblazers from Harriet Tubman with the Underground Railroad to Adam Clayton Powell, the first black person to become a U.S. Representative for the state of New York, to Madam C.J. Walker, who was the first black woman to become a millionaire, creating and selling her hair care products. I desired to join the ranks of these phenomenal black citizens.

Space and Aeronautics were huge topics of learning during the eighties, and I was a visionary. I would envision myself putting on a space suit and walking to the spacecraft, climbing in, being propelled from Earth to space, counting endless stars. The stars went on as far as the eye could see and beyond. I thought that was the coolest job ever and I wanted it. I grew up in a time where the sky was not the limit, what you dreamed of could be.

For many of us, it's about what we consume on a daily basis. We can either feed ourselves with negative information or assertive, positive affirmations. The latter is what my mother gave in our home, a woman who was a divorcé, single parent of three children.

Witnessing a constant badger of negative behavior from a friend's mother over thirty-five years ago, I've seen the results of that; a broken alcoholic woman on drugs with a mouth so dirty that it would put a sailor to shame. Being a mother, I knew that my role as parent and mentor was crucial to my son's success. I knew that what was instilled in him early on, would set the stage for his entire existence, and thus I protected and held that role as the most responsible position I could ever have. His very life depended on it.

My mother told me when I was younger, that I said I would have my own company by age thirty. To be completely honest, I don't remember that conversation, but that is what happened. My overnight success started at the age of 10 when a few other kids in the neighborhood and I wanted our own; we became partners. We would collect aluminum cans, cut grass with a non-motorized push lawn cutter, and babysat the neighbor's children. That was my first real experience as an entrepreneur.

An average student, I had to study to pass. We all know classmates who made it seem effortless to earn excellent grades. I was not one of those. Commencing from high school was non-debatable however. Attending college was expected but not required. I got my first real dose of denial when the first day of school was approaching in a few weeks, and the financial aid representative said that I did not have enough funding nor was there any time left to apply for loans and thus, I was not going to be attending my school of choice.

Devastated, I wasn't sure in which direction to go. As I conferred with a few of my classmates, I remembered that a few of us received full tuition paid scholarships to Dyke College, a private college in downtown Cleveland. Although I was grateful for the opportunity to be in college and only have to pay for books and other miscellaneous expenses, I still felt a sense of failure. We all believe that there is a road map of sorts that, if we follow, we will get to our desired destination. Life, however, will show you differently.

The goal was Attorney at Law! My alma mater offered several majors to choose from in the legal arena, so I preferred Paralegal. It would take five years to earn that degree, but I did it.

On Top of the World

I had no idea what a title or escrow company was, but I was fascinated by the opportunity to work with older professionals. I was like a sponge. I would come in early and be one of the last to leave. This career move was the most exciting move I ever made. I wanted to learn it all. Luckily, I worked with a group of men and women who loved their craft and was just as eager to teach me, this young grasshopper. I was twenty years old; the youngest by far in this office. I often unknowingly did silly things like heat up my lunch in the staff microwave, not thinking that the scent of smelly fish would stink up the entire office. Every goofy experience I had was preparing me.

My time there wasn't very long. I was laid off after only eight months. I believe my lay-off fell under the category of "Last one hired, first one fired." What was I to do? I was again feeling defeated; however, I knew that I learned enough to apply at another title agency, and thus I did. Not just another agency, but a leading national underwriter of title insurance.

I went in with confidence. I didn't know it all by far, but I carried myself like I did. I was hired. That was my first real learning lesson of exuding confidence at all times, even when you know you don't know it all, you must convince the employer that you will be the MVP (Most Valuable Player).

I was offered more than double what I was making just a few weeks earlier. Talk about excitement! I was twenty years old and appointed one of the top positions in my department, overseeing the production of my co-workers.

"What was I doing?" I thought. I've only been in the industry for less than a year, and now I'm supervising? "Wow!" was all I could say. My job was excellent I felt because I worked in one of the most prestigious buildings in downtown Cleveland at that time. I was supervising, I had wonderful co-workers, and I was making great money, especially for a twenty-year-old sophomore in college. I was on top of the world!

I'm Pregnant

As luck would have it, almost a year to the date I was hired, we got the news that the company was consolidating and moving our entire division to California. So here I was again, soon to be unemployed. But wait...things were looking up. The company offered all the employees the opportunity to move with the company or accept severance pay equal to six months of our respective salaries! YES! The pressure was off, and I could breathe, if only for a short while. I had time. Then, I got the news I was pregnant! I was pregnant! "What am I going to do with a baby?" I thought. I can't take care of myself, and I'm losing my job! My life blueprint design was not like this.

The consolidation was happening in stages. Our department was the last unit to be moved. By this time, I had already given birth to my bouncing baby boy. It was real; he was real! I was a mother, and I was excited, humbled and grateful to have such a beautiful, healthy child. No words can express the joy I felt when he would look at me with adoring eyes. There is nothing in the world like it.

When it was time to say our final goodbyes at this company that I had grown to love, it was very emotional. We had become a family and vowed to stay in contact. Many of us did, however, as time ticked on, everyone went their way. I decided to take my severance pay and stay home for a couple of months to adjust to being a new mom but also to make sure that my education was not falling by the wayside.

By 1998, I had a reputation in the industry. People knew me and knew I had skills. The industry was, relatively speaking, small. So, if you were good, you were known. Likewise, if you or your company were disastrous, the word flew like wildfire. Now employed by a major firm, I had endless opportunities. There were options. I could remain a senior escrow officer/assistant vice president at the downtown location, or I could transfer anywhere in the country where a professional position was open within the company. I could make lateral moves for experience or accept promotions for a larger salary and more benefits. My salary was the most I had ever made, and I was just getting started.

During this time, I decided to apply to law school. I was on fire! Everything was falling into place. I took the LSAT, prepared my application and essay, mailed it in and waited. "Denied." I was denied with a recommendation. The denial letter stated in part "That the application process is extremely keen," and then at some point in that letter, it was recommended that I pursue my Master Degree and reapply. That was a hard pill to swallow, but perhaps they knew something that I did not. So, I did what the letter stated.
I earned my Master Degree in Business Administration.

I Made History

The opportunity of a lifetime finally came. A lady with much more experience in the industry approached me about working with her on a new venture. She was creating a new escrow and title company and wanted me to manage it. I would have full control. In fact, I could hire my assistant and conduct the day to day operations without little to no interference from anyone. I was very interested. However, my goals at this point were set higher. Much higher I wanted my own.

After carefully negotiating and structuring our business transactions, we settled on me buying out her interest in the company after one year of me completely managing the firm. In 2003, I purchased Shaker Title Services Corporation making me the youngest black woman to own and operate a title insurance agency in the State of Ohio!

I was thirty years old. I was finally one of those trailblazers that I desired to be like and dreamed about as a youth. I could join the ranks of Harriet Tubman, Adam Clayton Powell, and Madame C.J. Walker. I got to speak with young people who looked like me, told my story as a means to encourage.

To let them know that no matter the situation of yesterday's, as long as you can dream it, you can achieve it. It was about giving others hope. This young black woman from the rough streets of Bridgeport Connecticut and Cleveland Ohio, respectively, raised by a single mother, who was also a single parent, could dream and accomplish.

It didn't hit me right away that I was now my boss. Because the business was already up and running, it was business as usual. I did however immediately notice the change in my income. Gone were the days where someone else dictated my salary and benefits. I was the boss, and I paid myself accordingly. My dreams were finally coming to fruition. Life was grand! I was in a position to build for myself and my son a half-million dollar five bedroom six bath dream home with all the works, including a chandelier lift in a beautiful suburban community! A chandelier lift? I had never heard of one until the builder introduced it to me.

I was always taught to diversify and as the opportunities presented themselves, I began to acquire real estate. Buying, renovating, selling, and renting over two dozen homes over the course of a few years. I was setting myself up for a great life and financial security. Nothing could stop me! I was a train on full steam ahead. No one could have prepared me for the next chapter of my life.

My Soul Rattled

"When life is going well, and you visualize these good things happening, you imagine more good things happening, that's easy. What's not easy to do is when things are going bad, and you're visualizing the right stuff." - Connor McGregor

That phone call from my mother at 6:30 a.m. on that cold January 4, 2007, morning rattled the deepest part of my soul. She said in a calm voice,

"Reesie, you're in the paper." As she read the article to me, I could see this dark cloud surrounding my life. It was the calm before the storm. The real estate market had decreased significantly. Lenders were shutting its' doors in rapid droves. The economy had begun to decline.

Something major was happening and apparently, I was in the center of it. I just never knew how much.

It was crunch time. I gathered my son for breakfast at the kitchen table after he dressed and was preparing for school. I wanted to speak to him about the news I received. I knew there would be whispers that morning because the staff knew me. I was active in my son's life and a regular staple at his school. Also, I loved the fact that each morning, you could walk into the front door of the school and grab the daily paper. Now, I dreaded that amenity.

Our diverse community was small; everyone knew your name. Consisting of eighty percent white to its twenty percent black and other population, yet there I was in black and white, "Real Estate Fraud." That bang at my front door changed my world forever. As I opened it, a Cuyahoga County Deputy said,

"Clarissa Foster?"

"Yes," I said, as my heart beat out of my chest.

"I have a warrant for your arrest." she continued. *"Turn around and place your hands behind your back."*

My world and everything in it went dark standing there looking at this camera as high as the ceiling taking this mug shot felt surreal.

"Face forward," the officer said. *"Turn to your right."*

Everything was a blur. How did I get here? What was happening? I was not in control anymore. A third party was choreographing everything that was going on.

Meanwhile, all hell was breaking loose. At the top of the news, a massive Mortgage Fraud bust consisting of sixty-seven people in Cleveland was being aired on every channel locally and even made the syndicated news. My life was over, I thought to myself.

Bail posted and taken home, I crawled into my bed with my son and stayed there for what seemed like an eternity. "What do I tell him?" I thought. I was not sure what was happening myself. The humiliation and embarrassment were just the top of the iceberg. "How do I explain this to my staff? What was the next step?" Everyone was looking to me for answers, to which I had none. Nothing in life had prepared me for this. The indictment consisted of dozens of charges ranging from multiple accusations of 'theft by deception' to 'receiving stolen property' and 'securing writings by deception.'

"WHAT the hell are they talking about? I am not a thief, what did I steal?" So many questions were swirling. My attorneys advised me to sit back and prepare myself for a long process.

Going back to my office was hard. My staff showed up, but no one knew what to do. We hugged one another. We cried. Then like clockwork, the phones started ringing off the hook. Everyone had questions. I did not have the luxury of breaking down again. I had to put my big girl panties on and handle business. After stepping into my office and closing the door, I sat down in my office chair. Taking deep breaths, I called my underwriter. "Do I still have a business?"

My Business is Gone

"Was I not a great agent for the company? Did not we pass our audit with the company only a few months earlier? Did not we just a week ago send them a huge remittance check? Surely, they would back me with the full strength and power of the largest underwriter in the United States." I thought. After a brief conversation, we agreed that we close whatever was in our pipeline and not take on any new deals until this case was resolved.

The realization was, 'Shaker Title Services' was closing. Although I had so much support and a few loyal clients who would stick with me through the process, I could not add to my portfolio, and I surely could not pay expenses for a firm that had no income. My dream fulfilled, was now dissipating. It was over, and my reputation in the industry shattered. Now, everyone knew my name, and it was like mud.

Guilty

"He who has a 'why' to live for can bear almost any 'how.'   – Nakia Thomas

The time had come after fighting the case for a year and a half, with multiple pretrial conferences and trekking down to the courthouse to sit outside the courtroom while the judge, prosecutors, and attorneys conferred, to a three-day trial, the verdict, *"GUILTY"* is what I heard over and over and over. **Guilty of theft by deception, securing writings by deception, and receiving stolen property for each title and escrow file in question.** All of this happening because a subprime lender's "professional witness" walked into a Cleveland courtroom with her sunny California tan, flowing blonde locks, and Jimmy Cho high heels clicking all the way to the seat adjacent the jury, sat and knowingly perjured herself in open court by swearing under oath that Argent Mortgage would never accept its' buyers using a down payment assistance program to purchase homes.

The only witness to testify against me as the President of my company. So, there it was. It really was that easy to find myself doing time for a crime that I did not commit. Or more importantly, never existed. Adjusting to life as an inmate was not easy by far. I was sleeping, eating, showering, existing next to rapists, murderers, and pedophiles. During this time, my only focus was on how I could get out of there. I wanted the life back I had before January 4, 2007. That life was long gone, never to exist again. Time waits for no one. The clock will tick every second until the end of time.

Two thousand twenty-two days! That is how long I was inmate number **WO73139.** I never thought I would see the day I was set free. The reality was, I knew it existed, but its' tangibility seemed unimaginable. What was even more frightening, what would I do when I was free? How would I be received? I know I had a love of family and a few friends, but how would the world treat me?

Many who have not known anyone to be in similar circumstances, judge. That is the reality of it. I am sure at some point in my life, I also judged others. It is human nature. Of course, my viewpoint has changed. I now know how easy it is to get caught up in situations that are beyond our control and end up in the worst position possible.

THE READY WOMAN

"In the end, she became more than what she expected.
She became the journey, and like all journeys, she did not
end, she just only changed directions and kept going."
                                        ~ author unknown

For most of my life, my name was synonymous with all things great. I was a great mom. I was a great daughter and businesswoman. I was a great friend. Then, I had my aha moment. "I AM still all these things. I am great!" I tell myself every day. I build myself up so that I can go out into this world and conquer it. Let's define the name. Clarissa derived from the Latin word Clarus which means "Bright, clear or famous," I realized that I am as my name says I am. I am bright. I am clear. I am famous. I speak those things into existence so that they will be. I live by the scripture that our Creator has for us; Jeremiah 29:11 "For I know the plans I have for you. Plans to prosper you and not harm you. Plans to give you hope and future." I also understand that "Faith without works is dead." So, as I count on my Creator to order my steps, I am doing my part.

Diary of a Ready Woman

I decided to renew my Notary Public license and pursue my dream of going to law school. Many asked what I wanted to do with that degree and license. Of course, practice Real Estate Law, what else?

"Giving up is never an option, not even a possibility," my wise mother would often say. "Is there an age that one could give up? Hell No!" If there is breath in this body, I shall pursue my rights of Life, Liberty and the Pursuit of Happiness.

About the Author

Clarissa Foster knew as a child she was destined for greatness! Growing up in the future home of the 2016 NBA Champs, Cleveland, Clarissa attended Jane Addams Business Careers Center where she studied Legal Secretary. Knowing that her aspirations were a lot higher, Clarissa pursued and earned her Bachelor of Science Degree in Paralegal from Myers College. While simultaneously working in her chosen career, Clarissa received her Master Degree in Business Administration from Myers University.

At the age of 30, Clarissa became the youngest black female CEO in the State of Ohio to own and operate an escrow and title insurance agency. The employer of over a dozen full-time staffers and independent notary closers, Clarissa's goal was to ensure that her firm, Shaker Title Services Corporation, was not only a leader in the industry but also held a reputation for quality of service and integrity of the products offered.

Clarissa is a contributing author of "Permission to Speak," a compilation of writings sponsored by the City of Cleveland. She also has refreshed her long-term desire to earn her Juris Doctorate. Distinguished honors include the A.B. Bonds Award from Baldwin Wallace College, The TRIO Achievers Award by The Ohio Association of Educational Opportunity Program Personnel (OAEOPP), Community Leader Recognition Award from the City of Cleveland Mayor Frank Jackson, and the Prosperous Young Black Women award. She is also a proud mother of one adult son.

ClarissaSpeaks216@gmail.com

https://www.facebook.com/clarissa.foster.505

Dedication and Acknowledgments

This book is dedicated to anyone who has experienced challenges that were or are seemingly insurmountable. There are plenty of examples of overcoming. I am living proof. Keep living. We are given these bonus days because our Creator says it's not over. Live! I am truly grateful to my mother Bettie Simpson known as Ms. Bettie for always feeding greatness into me. I am thankful to equally great women, like my mentor and dear friend Dr. Yvonne Pointer, for being a constant in my life, no matter where I was.

I am thankful to my sister Rameana Foster for holding it down during my absence. I am so grateful for my stepfather Rev. Willie Simpson for being an example of a great man to my son and our entire family.

To my best friends, Felicia Woods-Wallace, Tracie Grier Jackson, and Debora Cofer, who are more like sisters than friends, our friendship never wavered. And to my "counselor" Nasira Nekisha Michelle for being the creator of such an amazing project and thinking enough of me to insist that I be a part of it, I only say THANK YOU.

I am incredibly humbled. There are many other people, and not enough space to acknowledge. If you believe I am referring to you, I am.

THANK YOU, AND I LOVE YOU!

Personal Notes:

_____

_____

_____

_____

_____

_____

_____

_____

_____

_____

_____

_____

_____

_____

Diary Entry 4
The Wealthy Bitch
By Angela AJ Thompson

dear diary

It's me Angela...   *April 4, 1995*

The Accident

I wasn't trying to kill myself the day I ran in front of his car. I was just mad and wanted to shake him up, let him know how much he was hurting me. He was the person who, for 15 years, never wanted to see me hurt, but he was tearing my heart out piece by piece.

My husband blindsided, his car hit me

The truth is, he did not hit me. I ran into him. He was on his way to one of his whore's houses. That is what I called them: Whores coming from harlot in the Bible. By that time, it was just an in-the-open thing. He was no longer hiding his deeds; he was just straight up cocky.

"I am a grown man; I can do whatever the hell I want," he'd say. *"I work and I pay the mortgage. I do what I want and go where I want to go,"* he said before he left that night.

No more apologies, no cover-ups, just blatant cockiness. That day, I had a bad day at work. I was sick, the kids were sick, and he was hitting the streets. I think I flipped out.

I ran through the house, out the back door, and past the pool, through the gate, and into his car. He had just left all cleaned up,

75

smelling good for her. The other woman. Little did I know at the time that there were several of those other women.

I Was Adopted

I had both my adoptive parents and my biological mother because we were all family. I met my biological father much later, only then learning that he had begged to marry my mom and raise me. But, the perception he wasn't good enough was the barrier. The story told me was my mother went to college and came back pregnant with me. My fire-and-brimstone preacher grandfather was none too happy. His wife, a registered nurse and family caregiver, had died unexpectedly just two years earlier, and he had one daughter in medical school. He was determined to make sure each of his four daughters graduated college, so he had to come up with a plan. His sister and her husband could not have a child, so he arranged for them to adopt me.

My mother continued her college education, and before my grandfather died, she had received master's degree. Before he died, all his daughters had graduated college with graduate degrees, including the doctor, who graduated from medical school in 1968. I didn't hear my father's version of the story until much later.

Even with a ton of love from my family, I had a sense of loneliness. By the time I was fifteen, I had met my best friend and the man I was going to marry. When I turned eighteen, I enrolled in college using my maiden name. That was the last time I used it.

The Bitch

I'd known that it would only take him a few minutes to get through the subdivision and onto the street, and my timing was impeccable. He hadn't gotten up to full speed, and there I was, on top of the car. He stopped and got out.

"What are you doing?"

"Go ahead and kill me," I replied being the drama queen that I was.

It was the least he could do for me. He immediately turned into the kind, loving man that I had married. Just for a while. He helped me into his car and, without saying a word, turned the car around right on the two-lane street and took me home. He made a call and remained home that night.

That was the night that I realized I'd had enough. I felt fat, at a size fourteen, not because he told me I was but because society said so. I felt a failure because my marriage was falling apart because the church that I so loved told me I was.

That crazy night had started with a woman calling me a bitch. She called all the time and harassed me because my husband allowed her to. That evening when the phone rang, I picked it up, of course, this was before caller ID- I said hello, and she said

"Bitch put him on the phone; I need him."

I marched to my husband, mad and thinking that he would be mad as well. He had promised that he was going to stop this woman from calling.

I handed him the phone, and not only did he not rebuke her for calling, but his dumb ass proceeded to tell the woman.

"Okay, I'll be there."

He jumped in the shower and continued to go. I begged him to stay home with his family. While he took, his time getting ready, I cried and begged... I prayed... I tried to pray over him. I believed in prayer. I had been in every prayer line in town, it hadn't worked before. The prayer worked this night, he stayed home.

There were several times that he stayed home and chose his family. One time, there was a major hurricane, and our daughter was crying,

"Daddy, please take us out of here the neighbors are already leaving."

Our son was paying no attention, as usual, and I was quietly panicking. He got a phone call, and I could hear the woman screaming through the phone:

"Where are you? I'm scared. The storm' is coming. The news is saying that this is a killer storm!"

"Why are you calling me? You need to get with your family and go to them. I have to get my wife and kids out of here."

"Well damn. Who wants to live a life where your lover can't be counted on to keep you safe?" I said to myself.

But then I asked myself who would live a life in which they're miserable except for a moment of pride here and there. That night was the night that I realized that I had either gone crazy. I knew that I was holding onto the days of happiness that we'd had, which had lasted over ten years and three children, one who died only hours old.

I will always remember the tenderness his father showed when he held his little lifeless body while I screamed. I also remember the pride he had felt when the first and third babies were born. The love that he'd had for his wife and kids was awe inspiring.

His love and level of kindness were the material that inspired love stories. To this day, this man treats me like his high school sweetheart, like he's done nothing to me.

Then there was the misery. I went through many years of suffering. Part of him was fun and very accommodating... he made sure I had the best home, buying us a new one. I always drove a nice BMW. I worked as a sales manager for a major company and used my money as I wished. I paid the electric bill and groceries only. The children had the best we could afford, and we had more than one savings account. By the time each child turned sixteen, he had a car.

The cars were not new, nor fancy, but they were nice ones and paid in full.

From the outside looking in, we were a model family. Other than him turning himself periodically into 'Captain Save-A-Whore.' You see, he only chooses weak women that were down on their luck- The one that named me "Bitch" worked at Dillard's department store and had to be dropped off and picked up at work. The last one that I kept track of works at the Belk's store, but he helped her get a car. I guess the dropping off and picking up got to be too much for him. Nevertheless, his attraction was to less than-ambitious women, while I constantly tried to better myself.

After the accident, I cried myself to sleep in his arms as he apologized and promised to change, which I knew was a lie. He was having too much fun! I knew then that I needed a plan to at least have some choices. I decided to build a plan to become wealthy.

I thought people would feel sorry for me when I tried to share that I had a problem and what it was. Our life was looking good on the surface and him being nice, made me look crazy. As for the "real" story, only family, friends, his whores, and Mrs. Greenbaum knew the truth.

How Much Money Do You Have?

Mrs. Greenbaum was a friend of my great aunt. She was twenty-five years older than me and had no children and few relatives. I later realized that she paid so much attention to me because the family she had left paid no attention to her. Perhaps they were a little put off by her. She was the quintessential nosy Jewish women, who could ask you questions in rapid-fire fashion. You couldn't lie because the next question would make you incriminate yourself. I called her Ms. Elizabeth, and she called me Ms. Angela. We talked every month, and it was my time to laugh. I always laughed. I also could purge myself and only tell the truth.

The week after I jumped in front of the car, I spoke with her and told her that I had gone crazy and decide to leave. She explained to me that I wasn't crazy, I just needed to change my mind. That day, I changed my plan to stay. She started by asking me how much money I had.

I proudly said, "Ten thousand dollars' liquid and fifty in my 401k."

"How far would that take you if you lost your job young lady?" she laughed.

"I thought you were going to say a hundred thousand, at least. Why don't you focus on making it to a hundred thousand? Concentrate on a million. I see you as a millionaire."

She had no idea she was repeating a prophecy my great aunt had made a year before.

"Well, there is child support and alimony," I said.

Her reply was simple. "Silly girl, you have been ambitious, you make too much for alimony, and the child support will run out. Is he beating you?"

"No, of course not! Why would you say that?"

"You act like it, the way you are trying to leave. Back in my day, they all cheated. They would go to 'play cards,' but that is NOT what they were playing. We women shopped, lunched and decorated.

I had to interject, "I am not wealthy, and I cannot shop or, lunch, and I certainly cannot even afford to redecorate."

Elizabeth raised her voice. "LOOK! Find something else to do. Better yourself, ignore his dumb ass. You said you wanted your kids to have a two-parent household, make it happen! Stay there, build up your money, focus on yourself, educate your children, and realize your dreams, all with him helping you."

I did just that. That day, I put my plan in motion. I turned off the emotions. I was sweet but guarded. I told myself that the man that I fell in love with and married had died. That may sound harsh, but it was how I got by. That was my only tactic. I loved him and always would, so what else could I do?

When I tell you I paid no attention to what he did, I am serious. I allowed those sad, ignorant women to argue and fight over him. One woman was retired military and married. Why she fussed and fought over another married man, I just couldn't figure out. I did read his texts; they brought me comic relief.

The women cried and begged over and over. The one in South Carolina just acted like she would die if she couldn't be with him. She was what you would call a 'paymaster' she bought him clothes, jewelry, anything. Mrs. South Carolina probably would have bought for the kids and me if I had asked. It was crazy.

I can see a woman being emotional if she is married to a man, and maybe if she's the mother of his children, but these women fought to the bitter end over a married man that was not loyal to his wife but apparently was not with them either.

If they were such a big deal, there would not have been two or three at a time. My story is not one of getting mad and leaving. Mine is one of staying with someone that was compassionate to me on many levels to be secure and ultimately successful. I had a plan, and now I have success!

The Million-Dollar Woman

To quote Shakespeare: "To thine own self be true." I plan on being true to myself at all costs now. I am incredibly grateful for the lesson. My goal became bettering myself and fulfilled the million-dollar prophecy. Every day, I woke up and asked God for the wisdom to go forth and meet my destiny, and for many years, I heard no response. I kept asking.

I kept reading, and I can genuinely say I am stronger because of the wisdom of Ms. Greenbaum.

I buried Ms. Greenbaum, as well as many of my close family members. I still got stronger. I was empty for a while, wondering when things were going to change. Eventually, I realized that change doesn't come overnight, no matter what you do. But it will come. The key to my success was straightforward. Compartmentalization. Everything is complete and categorized according to the order of importance in my life. It includes both goals and issues. Nothing changes the priorities.

One day, my daughter called and said both her nose and her finger were bleeding.

"Use a Band-Aid on your finger and some tissue in your nose. I have to make a business call. I will call you back."

I still have not called back on that issue. I am truly sorry, but she was grown by this time, with her own home. What was I supposed to do? That example is a harsh one, but an example of my ability to compartmentalize.

I also learned that people could not help you beyond what they know. Even the most educated person cannot teach you to be a business owner, they can only give you advice that they read from a book or, like most folks, which pulled information out of their ass.

Today, I am the CEO of a successful asset management company that I started ten years ago, in the height of the foreclosure crisis. Before that, I was a regional sales manager for the home improvement division of a major chain. I was using rental properties as an investment, but always praying for direction, for success.

A friend who was working in the banking industry suggested that I had the core competency to start an REO (bank-owned property) management company. We have begun out by cleaning out foreclosures, my husband even helped on the weekends.

My daughter was in high school, and even she assisted in those early years. Eventually, I took 50k out of my 401k and leveraged it to change the direction of the company. Once the company changed, it went from LLC to INC, which included a board and company shares.

We now have thirty-two subcontractors, predominately general contractors, as our focus is the rehabilitation of the electrical, plumbing, roofing, etc. At last look, we cleared nine point something million in a year. Not too bad for something that started out of a dream.

I am now the VP of a small property investment company. I am a VP of a nonprofit. I hold a real estate license, which I use for upscale clientele only. I am excited. I create excitement. An up and coming dating site. My new source of excitement.

Along with everything else that I do I am back to my passion: fiction writing and motivational speaking. I am aware that I cannot save the world, but I can certainly inspire it. My name is Angela Jones Thompson Remember my name. You will see it out there in publications and events. If you, like the lady years ago, decide to call me a bitch. Please add "wealthy" and "happy" in front of it!

He Asked Me If I Was Ok

This story is one of many, some less severe, some more. At one point, I started traveling and just never went home. The children were gone, and my husband and I had become roommates and friends. He continued to take care of me, even after I was making well into six figures.

He asked me if I was ok financially and then waited another year before we split to give me time to be completely whole. Then he bought a house and put my name on the deed and moved in. (This means if he dies it is all mine.) For all of that, I will be eternally grateful. We are now working on being friends again.

With thirty-five years of history and family, it is a much-needed step. I asked him recently about a few of those women. The married one that tried to buy him is back with her husband, who is now a minister in a church. She called him just six months ago and asked if she could come to Florida so they could have 'fun.' He said that he turned her down. He said he felt disgusted that she even asked after she and her estranged husband had reconciled.

It's possible he only felt that she was just too old. Who knows, he could have just been grossed out. She was seven years older than him, just like the one that called me bitch. He was into older women then. By the way, the woman that called me a bitch is still living in a rental home and working assisting mentally challenged people with their daily needs. Still no car. Probably still no morals. Did I mention she was deeply religious? Yep, that.

Maybe if the focus of those women had been on themselves, and in some cases their children, they would have fared a little better. None of them are what you would call wildly successful, but just like everyone, they still have a chance to succeed.

THE READY WOMAN

The truth is, I still have nightmares. Every occasionally, I will wake up in a cold sweat after a dream fight with my ex-husband or one of his women. No matter what drives your success, it could take a piece of your soul. Don't feel sorry for me. Like everyone, I must go through the healing process.

And, the dreams are a real inspiration for the award-winning fiction I write. Anyway, I always win in those fights and thank God; I do wake up and you will too. Don't be a fool, create a plan, don't waiver and know that what you want is possible.

About the Author

Angela Jones Thompson raised in Florida in a small town with one stop light, the child of an educator. The experiences she gleaned from her small-town roots gave her the confidence that she could achieve anything she wanted! Even though life took several interesting turns, Angela, as a CEO of a successful asset management company. A VP of a Real Estate investment company and a business development investor. The CEO of marriagemindedonly.com Angela is also a record producer with her first contribution on **"Lift"** from award-winning artist **Akia Uwanda.**

Angela has a knack for inspiring people to live their best life! She was later focused on her success and finds joy in encouraging others to do the same. Angela uses methods for motivational speaking via funny small town stories to serious, "Get off your butt and make it happen type talks! She also created "Chats with Angela" An opportunity for those who want to have a no-bias conversation with a sister/friend.

Angela spends her spare time traveling. Traveling, you can see her pop her laptop out and work on something. Other than a passion for work and business development and writing, what truly makes Angela happy is the laughter of her adult children.

www.angelajthompson.com
www.facebook.com/angela.thompson.9047
www.instagram.com/theajthompson/

Dedication and Acknowledgements

To Bertha White who never doubted my ability to SOAR! To: Andrea Thompson, Rick Thompson, Richard Thompson who each showed me that I could indeed Love unconditionally.

To my Creator which has never failed to come through....

Personal Notes:

_____

_____

_____

_____

_____

_____

_____

_____

_____

_____

_____

_____

_____

_____

Diary Entry 5
Companion of Fools
By Amber G.

dear diary.

It's me Amber...   *January 17, 1995*

A Man I Didn't Want

Having been forced into a hell, I can attest I believe he would have killed me if he hadn't dropped his gun. The police were on site escorting me to the ER. My neighbor saved my life; instinct had him swooping that weapon up. He didn't have to get involved; I can't say I would have been brave enough to do the same. Why I acted a fool over a man I didn't even want was beyond me and why I believe in Karma. I received three layers of stitches to reduce scarring: 19 in all, eight on the outside, five in the middle, and six inside my lip. Let me explain how I went from one hell of mental abuse to another of physical violence.

You Know I'm Going to Marry You

Way back before the drama 'Army Wives' became popular; I had my own episode going. As a junior in high school, my family moved from Denver, Colorado to Columbus, Ohio. So here I was in a new state and new school. Many of the girls grouped in cliques, were not willing to invite me to the social events or speak to me unless they were being nosy.

On the other hand, I had lots of attention from the guys. I had my pick of guys to choose from, but this one guy—I'll call him Sean—was the life of the party.

"Hey Amber, did you use to ride horses to school in Denver?" Sean clowned me one day at school and the class roared with laughter.

"Boy please, Denver is a little more gangster than you think." I retorted.

I didn't get offended because he was so funny. Sean kept me and everyone around us in stitches, telling jokes and just being a clown in general. It was refreshing; we had fun together.

We talked about everything when he walked me home from school even though he lived on the other side of town. He would catch the public bus home. We were inseparable; we were the Bobby and Whitney of our school. Sean wasn't a stud, but his personality more than made up for it and then eventually I thought he was kind of cute. Then he got a car and drove me everywhere. He was so kind-hearted and helpful to me.

"You know I'm going to marry you one day." He put a tiny diamond ring on my finger, and my mother called it an iamond... she removed the "D" jokingly because the diamond was so tiny. But I loved that ring it was genuine and from his heart. By my senior year, I was pregnant and trying to figure out how we would take care of a baby.

"What are we going to do, Sean?" I paced the floor until I wore out the threads in my socks. "I'm going to join the army," Sean announced.

That November I had the baby, and in the Spring, he went away to boot camp. Now that he had plans for his career, I decided I was going to move back to Denver and raise my child as a single parent.

One afternoon I had a conversation on the phone with Sean:

"I love you, why did you leave Ohio? I'm only doing this because I want to marry you and be a family with our daughter. Amber, will you marry me?"

I was stunned this was the happiest day of my life. "Yes, I will." I loaded my car up and moved back to Ohio.

We planned our wedding, but when I found out he would have to leave for a one-year hardship tour in Korea right after getting married, I fell into a depression. I was still a single parent. That wasn't the only problem while he was in Korea, I found out I was pregnant again. I was hurting emotionally, I just wanted him to be around to watch our children grow.

We talked whenever we could talk about our lives in long letters; it was costly to take long distance calls back then. We discussed how we missed each other and how Sean missed our daughter. We had plans after he finished his tour he would bring the kids and me wherever he was assigned.

Little did I know while he was away our vows to be faithful were already falling apart. When his tour was over, he lived in Washington State. One evening we chatted on the phone:

"Hey babe, so when can I come out there?" I questioned.

"I'm working on it, I just don't have the money right now, but when I file the taxes, I should be able to."

"Hurry up I miss you," I exclaimed.

He kept pushing the date back on bringing me out there saying he didn't have enough money or whatever he could say to prolong the situation.

My Heart Dipped into my Stomach

One time our baby boy had pneumonia, and I needed to get in touch with him. I kept calling the base; they would say he wasn't there. I remembered a few times when he called me he would say he was at a friend's house for the weekend.

The soldiers hated staying on base over the weekend and would often stay with friends who had houses off base. His friend was married; he explained his wife was also in the service.

I grabbed my phone bill to locate the number and call him at their house to tell him about our sick baby. I dialed the recurring number on my phone bill, and a lady answered. That didn't bother me; I believed she was his friend's wife.

"Hi, do you know Sean Jones?" I asked cautiously. "I need to speak with him." She let off what sounded like an exasperated huff.

"Hold on." was all she said.

I had a funny feeling about this. My heart dipped into my stomach. In the background, the mystery woman who answered the phone spoke his name softly like she was waking him up as if he were right next to her. Not like a guest in another room.

"Hello." He answered his voice groggy from sleeping.

"Sean, who was that?" I asked.

But as soon as he heard my voice, he hung up on me. Oh, hell no, I thought to myself. How was this happening to me? We never even had an opportunity to live together as a married couple. After I cried all the tears I could, I knew I had to get out there and save my marriage.

After I got my son well, I asked my mother-in-law to watch my kids so I could save my marriage. I bought a one-way ticket to Washington State. When I got there, I talked to my husband's Sergeant who promptly made him set me up in an apartment and get a car. My timing was impeccable; I got there the day after he received the income tax refund. I only found out because I had to sign the check for him to cash it.

"If you don't get a job today, I'm sending you back home," Sean barked.

"You're not sending me anywhere." That day I came back with two jobs.

Who was this man? I didn't recognize my husband; he was smoking and drinking. This wasn't the same guy I married. He was short with me, and it seemed like I interrupted his fairy tale life with the real one he was supposed to be living.

The Army Wives

One Saturday I was cleaning up and came across a duffle bag. I unzipped it expecting to find dirty clothes but instead, I found a pair of panties and pictures of him in what looked like a skiing trip with the same woman I assumed had answered the phone.

I discovered that instead of staying at a friend's house on the weekend as he told me he was living with her, which is why he couldn't move me out there. Not only that, I found out his mother was in on it. She and his mistress spoke on the phone regularly. But I didn't give up; I mean sure, he was a man, right? My marriage failing had to be happening because I wasn't around. I figured everything would go back to normal between us once I was with him again.

We needed time to get our Bobby and Whitney back, so I worked hard when I got there because I wanted to have my kids with me so we could be a family.

Soon our place off base became the place to be on the weekend for the soldiers who didn't want to stay on base. Friday night would roll around, and we had three or four guys who came over on a regular basis. I opened the door "Hey sis," they hugged me one by one.

"Where's my husband?" I questioned, they all shrugged. I built a bond with some of those guys. Later that evening one friend pulled me aside.

"Sean is still seeing ole girl; I'm pretty sure he's over there now."

"Thanks" was all I could muster, although I was livid inside.

Soon they were at it again. She called the house and hung up if I answered. That was a signal for him to call her. One day after getting off work early, I wanted to surprise Sean so I went to the base only to find him and her eating Chinese food together. That was supposed to be me eating food and chattering with my husband like a schoolgirl. I wanted to fight. I wanted to smash that Chinese food in both of their faces. She might not have known about me in the beginning, but she knew about me now.

By this point, I was sick of my emotional status: "It's complicated." My self-esteem was lower than a snake's belly. I couldn't understand it; what I was doing wrong? I was beautiful, sweet, and a genuinely good person—not to mention the mother of his children. But "who would want me after having two kids by someone else" was why I stayed and tormented myself.

Sean began to treat me so bad that on several occasions, he came in from work on Friday saying he was going to check the mail disappearing until it was time to go back to work on Monday running in with enough time to get dressed and head right back out. Other times I would be stranded at work because he wouldn't pick me up. There were many days I was stranded and forced to walk or accept rides from strangers.

One day I called my job at McDonald's crying

"I'm sorry, I can't make my shift. My husband hasn't shown up to take care of the kids so I can get to work. I don't even have milk or diapers for my baby," I blurted out my voice cracking, tears streaming my face.

We Watched Out for Each other

About an hour later, there was a knock on my door. I opened it, eyes red and face swollen from crying. My manager from McDonald's, no questions asked, handed me a gallon of milk and a pack of Pampers. I swear every time I think about that I get teary eyed. I felt mentally exhausted; perfect strangers had more humility for me than my husband.

So many nights I stood in the window my arms folded in front of me for hours on end waiting for a no-show husband. However, it was now, and I built an alliance with some of the other army wives having some of the same problems with their men. We watched out for each other, helped each other with our kids and kept our ear to the streets for any mess going down with our husbands. Like the time a friend of mine's husband was over some woman's house, we rode over there to confront him next thing I knew she threw a huge rock at his car.

"Come on girl," I yelled, I was the getaway driver that night we laughed and laughed. It's funny because, in boot camp, the Army brainwashes the men that Jody's got their girl. But what they need to be teaching the wives is that Jody's got their man.

On another occasion, my friend also an army wife from West Virginia was fed up too.

"Girl I'm sick of this; I'm going home. For real, you should consider going back too. I will drop you off in Ohio." My friend Shirley Thomas said.

"You would do that for me? You just don't know how tired I am of crying myself to sleep, why do I have to be married but alone." Hell, I was probably the poster child for Tyler Perry's movie, 'I Could Do Bad All by Myself.'

Shirley and I packed up her car and left. It felt like the perfect plan as we drove back home together. With my newfound strength and moving on attitude, my husband finally took notice of me. I was back on the market; I was no longer worrying about what he was doing. After Sean realized I moved on from him; he wanted me back. My primary objective was always to be a family, so I decided to give it another try.

We'll Be a Family

"I'm ready to get out of the service," he said. "I'll come home. I'm willing to be a better husband, and we'll be a family with the support of our friends and relatives." He assured me.

We planned for me to return to Washington until he could get out the service which was only a few months away and we would start our lives together with a clean slate. Things were better for a while even after we moved back to Ohio, but soon his old habits resurfaced.

I remember one Sunday he came home after being out all night. I was mad, he and I were play fighting but that moment I found a hotel key in his pocket... I lost my air. All along I knew deep down something wasn't right, but I tried to put those thoughts to the far reaches of my mind yet this was confirmation that I wasn't crazy.

That was the day I walked away from my marriage, the car, the furniture and the apartment for good. Not even a week later he was riding around with a pair of baby shoes hanging on the car mirror, not my child's shoes. One day I took our kids to his mother's house, and another woman brought a baby for his mother to watch. I later found out the baby was my husbands. He got someone pregnant while we were married. I tried so hard to hold my head up then, but I felt betrayed. I was a failure at marriage. I was a young, black woman with no college education, no backup plan, and two kids.

I didn't want to go back home to my parents and be an even bigger failure, so I moved in with a girlfriend of mine who later introduced me to her neighbor.

We hit it off, and soon I moved in with him. He seemed nice. He would cook for me, and we hung out and watched movies a lot. Soon he was buying me sweat suits, beautiful silk robes with matching gowns. I can't lie, he hooked me. I'd never been pampered by a man before.   However, it wasn't until we went out in public, I realized he had no class. One time we went to a restaurant:

"Yeah, let me get a Gin and Juice," he bellowed out to the waitress.

"That'll be one Gin and OJ," she repeated. But a confused look sat on his face.

"She means Gin and Orange Juice, not O.J. Simpson," I said rolling my eyes. (This was around the time O.J. Simpson was on trial.) It was apparent in public that we were not socially compatible.

I'm Not Cheating

It didn't take me long to figure out I was in a rebound relationship. I wasn't in love. I found out this guy was cheating on me too. Like the night, I picked the phone up off the receiver and heard him having phone sex with a female. I slammed the phone down letting him know he was busted.

"I'm not cheating; I was just bored."

But deep down I knew this was exactly the ammunition I needed to get out. One day I watched him dial his voice mail, and once I knew the password, I called it.

"Yes, this is the Days Inn in Cincinnati, you forgot your radio in your hotel room."

Hmmm, we hadn't been to Cincinnati much less at a hotel. Another cheater and liar. That day I went on and on about how he betrayed me.

"You're no different than my husband I just left. You're a dirty dog just like the rest."

I had become well versed when it came to talking smack. But I must have said dirty dog one too many times because suddenly, I was looking down the barrel of cold … hard … steel… his gun. There was a scowl on his face. I can recall the sick feeling of bile rising from the pit of my stomach, the sweat beads trickling down my brow. My kids ran into the room hearing the escalated voices.

"Mommy," I still remember the looks on their faces, how their slanted eyes turned as big as plate saucers.

"Go back to your room."

I tried to say calmly hoping the situation didn't escalate any further. All the while visualizing this story on the six o'clock news. Woman and children found murdered overnight. Everybody seemed frozen in place for what looked like an eternity. Realizing he pulled a gun on me in front of my kids, he backed down.

Why Didn't I Give the Key Back?

Almost as if on cue he started having seizures after that and even though I wanted to leave, I wasn't a cold-hearted person. The guilt consumed me; I didn't want him to think I was leaving because of his illness. But I wanted out, so I found a little house to rent, but my dad talked me out of it.

"This neighborhood is too dangerous," he replied, shaking his head no.

Neighborhood dangerous? Heck, I was already sleeping with the enemy. One thing I have learned over the years is to trust my gut instinct. I should've followed my heart and moved out, maybe things wouldn't have escalated the way they did. But instead, I waited around until I got myself a car, found an apartment and then I moved out.

"I still think of you as my lady, keep the door key."

Why didn't I give that door key back? I wasn't planning on using it; however, one evening I went to his house to get the rest of my stuff I left behind after I moved out. I went to use my key, but the chain was on the door. I looked through the crack of the door a woman was sitting on his couch. I let my female ego get the best of me. I felt like a fool, locked out with a key. Ha! Of course, you know I had to show my butt! I banged on the door.

"Let me in! Just let me get my stuff, and I'll be out of your life! That chick can have your sorry behind!"

That door swung open so fast it caught me off guard. He rushed me pushing me with all his might off the icy porch. "Ahhhhhhh," I yelled letting out a blood-curdling scream, I hit the ground face first. My face hit the ground so hard I felt my teeth click. Mmmm, I moaned trying to move my face I immediately recognized the horrible metallic flavor in my mouth. Warm blood oozed down my chin decorating the snow with crimson red droplets.

"Don't you ever come over here starting shit, where's my gun?" He shouted. Going back inside his apartment. I felt his neighbors swoop me off the ground and into their apartment. We heard several gunshots before he jumped into his car and sped off.

Once we believed he was gone, I rushed out to my car and drove full speed to my apartment. Inside I almost fainted when I saw the hole in my face. Looking into the mirror, I tried to open my mouth, but my chin and teeth were bloody.

"I need to get to the hospital, I need stitches," I told myself.

That's when I heard a commotion, which sounded like my front door was being kicked in. With my blood leaving a visible trail of my whereabouts it was impossible to hide, but I grabbed the cordless phone and hid in the closet anyway, I dialed 911.

Who Was That Nut?

"Someone is breaking into my house," I said and laid the phone down. My hands were shaking so badly I had to sit on them. I held my breath fearing he would hear me. I didn't know what I was going to do if he opened the closet door. Would that be it for me? Would he shoot me? Would I see my kids again? Tears burned my eyes in anticipation of the unknown, and I heard my name.

"Amber," he hollered. I heard him running up the stairs. I closed my eyes bracing for the impact.

This is it. I thought.

Suddenly it sounded like he turned around. I waited and nothing. I practically jumped out of my skin when I heard the gunshot! But the gunshot was outside.

"What the...?" I whispered to myself.

I tiptoed out slowly and looked down the stairs. My front door was hanging off the hinges. I slowly walked down the stairs fearing the unknown. I saw my neighbor when I reached the bottom.

"Is he gone?" I gurgled trying to cover my gruesome mouth.

"Yes, I don't know if I shot him or not?"

"I was just investigating all the noise from him kicking in your door when I saw a gun lying here in front of your doorstep. I snatched it up; when he realized he must have dropped it while kicking in the door, he ran back down to get it. I went into my apartment and shut the door, then he started kicking on my door. When it finally gave way, I shot at him with his gun that I had picked up. Who was that nut?" he asked.

You Don't Have to Get Married

I remember before getting pregnant mom saying don't come home pregnant, it was more like a threat never the conversation to explain why. You should speak to your kids with clear intent on what is happening because they don't know how to make rational decisions on their own. I remember another conversation with my mom:

"Amber, you don't have to get married just because you're having a baby, you can still go to college and live your life." But I was convinced I had all the answers.

"Just because your first marriage didn't work doesn't mean mine isn't going to work." I spat.

THE READY WOMAN

I was hard-headed, only learning after bumping my head. I often wonder if something or someone other than my mother would have intervened would I have listened? Years later I apologized to my mom, and now I value her opinion and often ask for advice before making decisions. What this all boils down to is that being a teenage mother led me down a path I might have been able to get away from had I not felt compelled to stay in that situation.

I was finally at a point in my life where I enjoyed my independence I wasn't worried about being with someone. I was enjoying my life as a single mother, working hard, traveling, and taking care of my kids.

One day a friend asked me to go to a party I wasn't feeling well, but she begged me to go. The birthday boy was surrounded by women all night I never gave him a second thought, but the next day my friend said guess who wants your phone number.

We worked together in the fast food industry years earlier as teens and had several mutual friends. We connected, and after dating for four years, we married.

About the Author

Amber G. is the author of the compelling series "Mergers and Acquisitions." In her second self-published novel "Game Faces On M&A2." Her mission is to write about characters who examine their lives, their hopes, fears, and motivations. Characters that will linger with you long after the story is over. She dreams that one day Mergers & Acquisitions the series will become an internet sensation or motion picture.

Working a 9 to 5 by day and author by night she hopes to one day make it a full-time job.

Amber G. currently resides in Ohio with her husband where she is a full-time mom. Armed with an Associate's Degree in business management and minor in leadership she's following her real passion by working on her next novels *"Mixfits"* and "Dreams Under Construction" part three of the "Mergers and Acquisitions" series.

As the president of the Ready Woman Society, she believes that success lies in the journey, not in the destination. There's more to learn during the process than in the promise. She encourages healthy self-esteem, attitude and woman empowerment. Being a jack of all trades, she loves to dabble in art, design, movies and of course reading. She's an active member of the Mahogany Writers Exchange.

www.booksbyamber-g.com

www.facebook.com/booksbyamberg

www.instagram.com/booksbyamberg

Email : booksbyamberg.com

Dedication and Acknowledgements

First, let me thank God for all His Grace, Mercy and Provisions during one of the roughest times in my life. Thanks to my immediate family, my circle I love you. This project would have been impossible without Nekisha Michelle and each one of my colleagues for their excellent collaboration thanks.

Amber G.

Personal Notes:

_____

_____

_____

_____

_____

_____

_____

_____

_____

_____

_____

_____

_____

_____

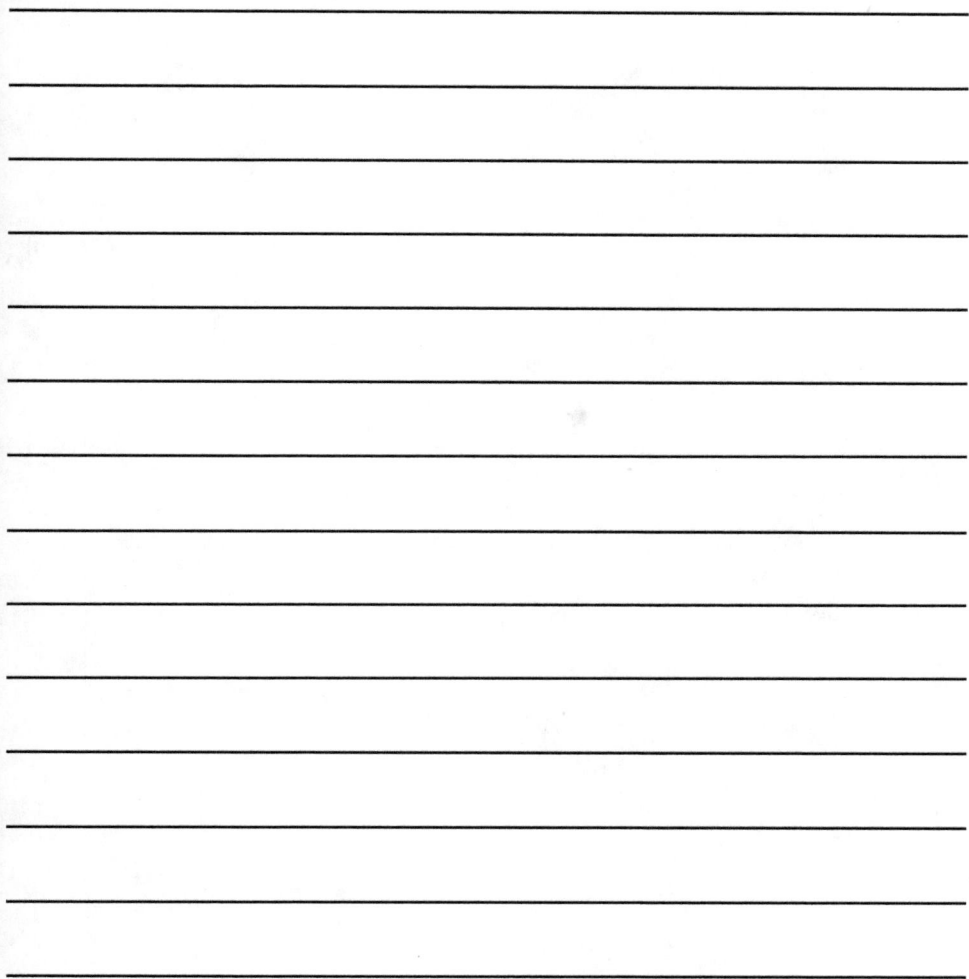

Diary Entry 6
All Tied Up
By L' Divine Holland

dear diary

It's me Leslie...   *December 7, 2000*

The Preview

I was pregnant about seven or eight months by Mister, the man I loved and believed loved me. He came to visit, and after not seeing him for the prior three months, we had sex. We role-played, which he loved to do—at least that's what I thought we were doing. Part of his game was picking me up off the ground by my neck, while spilling out demonic chants as he pretended to be Satan. He hogtied me up where my arms and legs were pulled together from behind my back. Once I was tied up he called me all kinds of whores. He also threatened to shove a broomstick up my vagina as he waved it back and forth.

Then, when Mister was done, he left me there alone, still tied up. I could hear him next door through the thin walls of my apartment, talking with my neighbor while they were smoking marijuana. My neighbor asked him where I was; he replied:

"Next door all tied up." Really? I was in my home, alone, in agonizing pain, all tied up, for about 2 hours. This was the first time I realized, I was that woman in the abusive relationship that I had talked about. How did I get here?

I believe that Mister was angry about my job. It was just that, a job. One way that I made money. A legal hustle. I got in the Adult Entertainment Industry two years before I met him. Seeing that I had to raise myself starting at age 16, it's how I survived.

I had my twin sister, Sierra, and after my grandmother, who was raising us at the time, passed away, we were all we had. My mother went into rehab, and the caregiver she left us with was in no better shape to care for us than she was. There was nowhere for us to go, so we ended up homeless, bouncing around for two years, staying with friends and in hotels. Life made us adults quickly. We had to endure and stick together.

If a Man Ever Hit Me

It's crazy: I was one of those typical women who said, "I would never let a man put his hand on me. If my man were ever to hit me, I would leave him immediately." Then I became that very person. I never understood why a woman would stay in an abusive relationship. To be honest, I feel that unless you've been in an abusive relationship, you couldn't remotely understand.

I remember enduring so many different forms of ill-treatment. The stalking, him slapping the shit out of me just because, or maybe it was because of something I said during an argument. These are the excuses that run through my head. I really thought that the father of my child loved me because he told me so.

Then I thought maybe we don't realize we're victims of abuse. Maybe we all felt that we deserved it, or that it is ok, it's *"Standard"*. Or how about we think love is supposed to hurt because he says, *"I love you."* Yeah RIGHT! He may, but his love hurts! I did not know that I was being abused, battered, neglected, manipulated and all the above. That I was now part of the *"Them"* now *"We"*.

An Adult Entertainment Star

A friend of mine, who I refer to as "the recruiter", introduced me to a few producers, managers, and agencies when I was only 17 years old. I developed personal, friendly relationships with them.

I knew that he intended to recruit me as soon as I turned 18. I assured him that the "adult industry", was not the route I would take. It wasn't my interest, it wasn't mainstream. I'm better than that.

I told myself that there was no way I would have sex with strangers, it wasn't me. I was a good actress. I was extremely comfortable with my body and in love with the camera, so none of that was an issue. It just wasn't for me. I had two jobs, and I was going to school. As some time went by things got tough again and I felt like I was running out of options. As soon as I turned 18, I was offered a porn gig.

My first job was with my best friend, so it made it more comfortable for me, it was her first time as well, so it was fun. I was shy, timid and skeptical. I had no idea and did not understand the life-changing experiences that I was about to face. She didn't either, and ended up going back home to Chicago. It's been over two decades since I last saw her.

The person I was in my early twenties was far from the innocent character I played as baby Jessica from "The Jefferson's" or the little Girl scout and church girl. I was in my lifestyle. I did not care too much for relationships, and I was not looking for a man. The person I was seeing at the time wasn't quite the future husband, and that situation was already heading downhill. So, I just went on with my life.

My second time was with a male, it was more difficult for me. The money can be decent and fast, but not as much for blacks, unless they did it all. And that was not me! I mean, I was a teenager, who could make anywhere between $600 - $1500 at a time. I was homeless, but my promise to myself, was never to be on the streets. I made my money. The problem was, I also spent it, as fast as I made it. I would tell myself, "I'll just do one more scene", then I'm done.

I was 20 years old when I met Mister. I was having a real ball. No children, and not much responsibility. I partied and did whatever I enjoyed doing. I was an adult porn star and model! My resume, bragged of shows for BET pay per view;

I was in Snoop Dog's very first: Doggy Style" adult video; I graced the cover of 2 magazines, "Black Tail" and "Players Pictorial", and more in the adult industry; I was also a dancer. During that time in my life, I preferred and was genuinely sexually attracted to women. When I got pregnant with my daughter, I wanted out of the porn industry, but I found myself in and out for almost ten years.

I Enjoyed Being with Him

The day I met Mister, I was on my way to a party with a group of girls, to perform a dance routine. Two famous rappers were throwing the party and he was part of their work crew. I don't remember seeing him that night, I so was tired. We had arrived late, missed the party, and were on our way back to the car, when all the girls started talking about how I ignored him when he was trying to speak to me. That should have been my sign. The next day I talked to him on the phone, when one of the girls, played middle-man, and called him to connect us.

I got pregnant the first -time Mister and I slept together, and the "honeymoon" was over. We had four months of bliss. We stayed in upscale hotels, ate what we wanted, went where we wanted, we were together for two to three days at a time, then back at it a day or two later. I enjoyed being with him!

Once I had my daughter Nia, my sister, Sierra, got a place, and we moved in with her. Sierra had a son, name Brett, one year later; we were a family. On the other hand, Mister never wanted our daughter around. When he and I would spend time together, I would have to leave Nia with family. He wanted me all to himself, all the time.

Our nights were wild to say the least. I was into women, most of my porn scenes were with them, it was much easier, safer, and more comfortable. Mister thought I would be ok with bringing that into our relationship, I was not. Who would want to share the man they loved?

I remember him calling me, and asking me to meet him at our usual spot. It was a beautiful hotel, which happened to be a 2 -hour bus ride for me, but I was excited, so I grabbed my bags and left. I knocked at the hotel door, there was no answer. I knocked again. Mister opened the door, let me in, and there was a woman sitting on the bed. I barely entered the room, in shock, as my heart dropped to the ground, along with my bags.

Not even seconds later Mister started to undress the woman in front of me. He began to kiss her all over her body. I began to get teary, grabbed my bags and headed for the door. Before I could get out the door, Mister aggressively took my bags, threw them across the room, and tossed me to the ground. I cried. He cursed me, yelling things like, "porn hoe," "bitch," and "fucking lesbian." He then proceeded to open the door pushing me out along with my things.

I can't explain how I felt. Despite what I did for work, I loved him, and nothing else mattered. It was approximately 11 pm at that time, and I had a 2-hour bus ride back home. That night was just the beginning of many attempts of force, putting me in an un-willing situation to please his excessive sexual desires.

As a surprise, Mister got into the adult industry, himself, acting as a recruiter. He asked for my help because I've always had a great fashion sense and I had top connections. I rejected his offer several times, and in my opinion, he wasn't the type of businessman that makes one feel comfortable. Eventually, because I loved him, I gave in and decided to help him. I would assist by styling the girls hair, give and help pick wardrobe, and of course, helped Mister with my connections.

The time came when he asked me to do a scene through him. Why would I do that? I did a photo shoot first and a solo scene. Then I did a full porn scene, one I did not want to do and would have never done on my own. He kept my half of the money. I don't even know how I cashed my check! Later, I discovered that this went on with all the adult cast. He had been conning them too. That was my final film in the adult industry. Things got out of hand and Mister's whole little organization fell apart. He was banned from the industry.

That joyride I initially experienced in the porn industry was over. I didn't care about the money anymore, nor did I want anything else to do with it. Just like that, I walked away. I wanted to be known for something bigger, and more inspiring. Nia was growing up, and I had to lead by example. Yes, I know one day I'll have to face her. I cannot change what I did, but I was able to transform into something better.

I genuinely believe that much of the abuse by Mister was because I did porn. When we first met, he seemed thrilled, excited even about my work. The next moment he would thrash me with cruel words of disrespect. He was my personal, Dr. Jekyll and Mr. Hyde, so to speak, he always kept two opinions of me.

He Disappeared

While I was pregnant, Mister disappeared, I wish he had stayed gone, but he didn't, and when he came back, he took over my life, my space, my time, my everything. Many horrible situations went on in our relationship, especially after he moved in with my family and me.

I couldn't do anything alone. I lost my job because I allowed myself to believe his lies, that he would take care of everything. All I had to do was be with him and please him. Everything I owned, he treated as if it was his, without my permission. I had lost control of my home, my possessions and myself.

I remember asking him one day why he never watched or spent time with our daughter. Mister got upset and told me that he couldn't be around children. That stuck with me, and I didn't argue. There was only one occasion when he watched Nia; I had a class that day and no sitter. He took our daughter to his mother's house. That was the one, and only time he ever spent private time with my her, and the only time she ever saw her grandmother. Nothing was working out!

Living with this man was everything I never imagined it could be. In the beginning, I thought it was what I had always wanted, but with control, came the beatings. The last straw came when I got home from Thanksgiving shopping, and he locked me out of my room.

I broke into the bedroom his face was covered by the sheet. When I pulled the sheet from over his head, he got up and socked me on the side of my head. Before I could speak, he punched me on the other side of my head.

My twin ran into the room screaming, "Stop!" He looked as if he was going to hit her, but that was enough! I was done! "GET OUT NOW!"
I had spoken up for the first time, and I meant it. At first, Mister said that he wasn't going anywhere, but when he saw there was no fear in me, he left.

The police came. I thought my sister called, but found out that Mister had called them from a payphone down the street, using a glade name. I guess he felt as if he was covering his tracks. The cops figured this out and although he didn't get arrested, they advised me to get a restraining order. That was the LAST time that Mister ever stepped foot in my residence. For now, he was gone out of our lives. Everything started to come to my memory. The first time I was pregnant, and he hogged tied me, leaving me there for hours, gaged. Now, seven years later, would be the very last time Mister would ever lay a hand on me again. I said it and that I meant this time.

He Had Not Changed

One year later, he contacted me, saying that he had a new home and wanted our daughter, Nia and I to visit, that he was a changed man. I felt he had something up his sleeve, maybe he was testing my courage. His house was two hours away. I went, but I never let my guard down, and I would be sure to pay attention to the signs this time. I made sure I would not get weak by bringing to memory all the terrible things he did to me.

I remembered how I literally almost died, and he never showed up to visit me at the hospital, or how he did not show up for the birth of our daughter. The trauma, violence, verbal abuse, all of it, I knew he had not changed.

During the visit, he raised his voice, and began yelling at Nia. I did not think twice, I left my belongings, took my child, and we left. He was now a threat to my daughter, and I needed to be that tough cookie of a woman I use to know, before there was a Mister. It was a test, and I had passed. I found myself again.

THE READY WOMAN

What did I learn? I have two less❤️or myself and the victims. Pay attention to the signs they are always there. Do not deny the signs and listen to your gut instinct.

As for yourself and personal desires, follow them but do not become a victim of them. You always have a choice, think and absorb that before you make that decision. Keep God first. Believe it or not, I prayed, even more, when I was in the adult industry than I did before it. My faith was and is powerful, and I did not shy away. So, I was and even moreso now, always magically protected, blessed and given all I needed by the Lord.

People change when they are ready. Some people have psychological problems and cannot change even if they want to. DO NOT TRY TO FORCE ANYTHING. If it doesn't happen, it's not meant to be. Many times, we ask for something and don't know what it is that we are asking. I remember Mr. saying to me at the beginning of our relationship *"Be careful about what you ask for, you just may get it and what you get is not what you thought it would be."* He was right about that.

For family and friends, sometimes the abused may not realize what's happening. You would not understand, but continue to be there for that person through their hard times. The abuser will try to seclude the victim from their family and friends. Do not let that happen, stay active in the victim's life as much as you possibly can.

Let the abuser know that you are there. Do not put down but remind the victim of who there were before the abuse, they will remember and hopefully, one day wake up. My family and friends saved my life.

WHO AM, I TODAY?   I am here and great because of it. I work hard to make sure that my daughter does not travel in the same direction as Mr. I must remember that he is part of her DNA. And it can be a challenge.

Ten years later I can love again, Yes, I have changed, but it is for the better. I am not afraid, and I forgive. I am on a mission to share my story and many other stories to help empower people like you.

I am an entrepreneur, self-motivated women who learned from her lessons. I look to others to guide me to my successes.   I am grateful, I am blessed, I am a writer. And most of all *"I AM A READY WOMAN."*

About the Author

Leslie D. Holland, also known as L'Divine Holland. Leslie has one daughter age 16. She lives in Los Angeles California, and yes, she is originally from Los Angeles California. Born in the month of October (which would make her a Libra) on the 3rd to be exact, in the year of 1979.

Leslie went to Monroe high school in North Hills California, in college she majored in Screenwriting and directing, studied dance, music, and theatre. In 2003, she earned her certification in Massage Therapy in the city of Glendale. She is an athletic person and a team player. She participated in sports such as drill team for three years at Foshay Jr. high school, track and field at Monroe high school. She studied and trained in physical education and physical therapy.

Leslie is self-employed as an independent Massage Therapist of 15 years, hair stylist, poet, and actress. Leslie recently became a board member of the new family own business. Some of her great talents include cooking, modeling, acting, and the one which is her calling, writing.

Leslie has ten siblings, five in which she grew up with, three sisters and two brothers. Something unique about her is that one of the siblings is her identical twin sister Erin Holland. Leslie and Erin were child actresses playing on the famous America sitcom television show "The Jefferson's" swapping, playing the character of Lionel's daughter, "Baby Jessica."

Ldivineholland@outlook.com
www.instagram.com/leslie_d.divine/
www.facebook.com/leslie.holland.18

Dedication and Acknowledgements

First, I would like to acknowledge and thank the Lord 'GOD'; indeed, none of these words I could write without Him. In loving memory of my grandmother, Letha Warren. I would like to thank her for many great words that keep me healthy in times of need. I would like to thank the few others who have come to pass for their words which encouraged me to be who I am today.

Thanks to my family, my mother Deborah for believing in me no matter what. My twin sister Erin, you're always trying to help me, thank you. My one and only daughter Sinai and nephew Jalen, I love you. To my siblings, nieces and other nephews, thank you, and I love you. Thank you, Daddy, I would not exist without you. All of my family you are special to me and have contributed to a significant part of my life.

I would like to thank all my twin's friends. God sisters Bianca and Qiana, no matter how far, we are unbreakable. Church family and girl scout besties Shneka and Temeka, and of course I can't forget Michell and Rochell. All of you have been faithful friends from the beginning of all friends, and I love you all.

Thank you, Rick, Brian, Victor, Bill for being there for me in so many ways. Dewayne, Ty, AC, Trisha, Joe, Johnnie, Marv, Tomeekha, Rasta, Al, Coraline, John and anyone else that I did not get a chance to mention.

Thank you, LaVette for introducing me to this great opportunity and Nasira Nekisha Michelle for allowing me to have this great opportunity. Each one of you gave me a reason to move forward, to never give up and to be my best. I appreciate and love you all.

I would like to acknowledge myself for taking a stand. If there is anyone that I did not mention, it's because I don't want to take up all the space. So, thank you. Thanks, Victor R. for helping me believe in love again!

Personal Notes:

_____

_____

_____

_____

_____

_____

_____

_____

_____

_____

Diary Entry 7
And Then I Woke Up
By Kimberly C. Brown

dear diary

It's me Kimberly...   *March 6th, 2008*

My Aunt is Dead

I woke up in my bed, crying hysterically, screaming: "My aunt is dead! Oh, my God! Oh, my God!"

In my mind, I didn't know if I had already missed the funeral or how many days it had been since she passed. While in grief and thought, I felt a touch on my arm, and a voice from under the sheets said:

"Baby, it's okay; I'm here for you, and you got this." Startled, puzzled, but weirdly not afraid, I wondered, who is this dude? Why is he in my bed? And who the hell is he calling Baby?

He was the least of my worries at the time; I needed to check what day it was and call my mom. She didn't understand why I asked if I missed the funeral. No one understood what was happening to me at the time; hell, I didn't know either. But she assured me I was good, that we were leaving the next day as planned to travel home to New Jersey for the funeral, and my great-aunt's body had already made it there safely. Thank God! Now I can tend to the mystery man in my bed, I thought.

He heard me get off the phone and walked into the living room: Fine as a chocolate-on-a-stick, muscles all over, and naked as the day he was born, with a fresh shape-up, mmmm... (Side note: I love a man with a new cut.)

There was no way we had not done something the night before. But I digress... he chuckled as he told me there was no need to have called my mom, that he could have told me that information. Which made me think, this was not a one-nighter; he obviously knew me. I didn't even know his name to respond, ask, or say anything.

I started a conversation to get the info I needed, and I asked him if he was coming to the funeral with me?

"I thought you told me you didn't need me to go? But I can call off from work if you want me to."

"No, I'm good; my family will be there for support," I quickly replied. "How much do you love me?" I asked without even thinking about what I was saying. It was as if I was listening to words come out of my mouth that I could not stop myself from saying. What a moron!

He smiled and laughed, "Since the day I met your crazy ass."

"And how long has that been?" I asked. He paused, as to think.

"Has it been seven months yet? I believe that it has..." he continued, but by then I was already in racing thoughts. Seven months? How could I not know who he was? What was going on with me?

When I came home from the funeral, I did a disappearing act. Not my finest hour, but what was I supposed to say. We obviously had no issues that I knew of, except for the fact that I didn't know him. For us, less complication seemed best; that's what I told myself, anyway.

My Breaking Point

It had been some weeks after the funeral, I had been going through a series of issues, I got some advice to start writing things down that was happening to me, that was unusual, no matter how minute.

I had been working on my list for a month now. It consisted of things like frequent loss of keys, forgetting where my car was parked (to the point, I'm outside crying and walking up, and down the street; the last time I phoned the cops I thought it was stolen, they found it, parked around the corner. I dared not embarrass myself again). Purchases that I know I could not and would not have made, losing track of time (short and extended periods), forgetting conversations that I had (i.e., telling a coworker I would cover for her and never showing for the shift).

The obvious, meeting and being in a relationship I didn't remember having. SMH... This list was getting annoyingly long and harder for me to understand. Like any reasonable person in the web-md.com age, I decided I would figure it out on my own, my diagnosis was Alzheimer's. In my mind the worst way to go, for someone who was known to have the best memory ever, I was failing miserably.

Then it happened... I woke up one day, I literally came to, driving! Driving, on a highway! Where was I going? Where the heck was I, was the better question? I felt lost. And when and how did I get dressed to end up here? I was freaking out! Did I become a sleep-walker? What time was it? What is today's date?

I pulled over on the shoulder I-480, terrified and in tears, I knew no one would believe me or understand. If they did, secretly they would say I was crazy, and rightfully so, I felt like I was losing it! I called my friend, the guy I had and knowingly had been dating on and off for some years at the time. I frantically explained what was happening and ended it with, "I don't know where I am, I need help!" He told me first to call my boss because I was supposed to be at work, and was late, again. It was true. I don't know how I still had a job?

Once he got me back on track, he let me know he was worried, that although I had been seeing someone, she was more of a counselor, and that I seemed to be getting worst and maybe needed a different professional. I was starting to think the same thing.

The Diagnosis

I reached out to my Sister-Cousin, who held a double Master's Degree in Psych from Columbia, and I felt she could help guide me in the best direction. She said it sounded like I had been having issues with dissociation, and it was not to be taken lightly. She added her concerns, one being, I needed to see a professional psychiatrist and tell them that, this may be my issue. She assured me they would know what to do from there, that a simple test could determine her conclusion. What was dissociation? How did I get it? Why did I have it? Is Alzheimer's out the door? I guess that's a relief or was this more severe? How bad was this going to get? Webmd.com here I come.

After reading online researchers, tons of library books, studies on the subject matter, and even watching movies, I realized maybe she was right, and it was some form of "dissociation." She was not the only one to come to this conclusion but my counselor as well. The things she shared with me about our sessions were quite alarming, and by this time I had been seeing her for about two-three months. I was officially scared, nothing I read about this "Mental Health Disorder" made me feel at ease. And I was not at all happy with what that label implied about my mental status either.

I spoke with my pastor, and he pressed that if I was going to see a psychiatrist that it be a Christian one, and we were fortunate to have one at the church who could see me. I remember walking into her very tiny office; it was nothing like I thought it would be, you know, how they look in movies. It was tight, just large enough for her desk, and a small table for two, but for some reason it made me feel a little safe, seeing as I was about to tell her I was going crazy and expected her to say to me I was not. That was my prayer anyway. I told her what had been happening. The more I talked, the more severe her soft-spoken voice began to sound. She asked questions, then more and more questions. The more she asked, the tighter that room started to feel. I mentioned that I thought I was having issues with dissociation, and she quickly responded,

"Where did you hear this terminology? Why would you say this is what you are experiencing?" I told her about speaking with my cousin, also a professional and she noted it and nodded.

My second visit was even more intense than the first, trust me. There was no small talk this time; the therapist got right to business, you would think she was paying me for the hour, instead of the other way around. The questions she asked were starting to sound familiar; then it hit me, she had begun to do the test my cousin mentioned to me.

It was a series of questions, I had come across them in one of the library books. I took the test at home, and read the result, so I already knew where this was leading. I answered them all, and then she asked me two questions I will never forget. (1) "If you were to dissociate, right here in front of me, would I know?" Without hesitation, I answered, "No, I don't believe you would." She paused like she was searching for a response, but all that came was another question. (2) "What made you realize you needed to see me?" This time I did pause, I had not told her how I awoke on the highway lost. As I told her, her jaw dropped. I had done it!

I made the smile disappear from her face, and I had proven that I was insane. Before the session ended, she said she no longer wanted me to be a Nanny, that my mental state was not stable enough to attend to children. What? Nannying is what I do. Now I knew for sure she was crazy. I had never hurt a child in all my years of childcare, nor did I have any incidents or accidents involving children. I was the safest person I knew, and anyone could tell her the same.

Her diagnosis, labeled me with DID, Dissociative Identity Disorder, formerly known as Multiple Personality Disorder. Huh, come again! DID was not real, and not happening to me... But it was. The dreaded truth made it real, and now I needed to deal with the reality, but denying is easier.

The True Test

I didn't go back to see her ever again. It was not her fault, but she did just give me the most depressing news of my life, behind my grandmother's death in 1996. Besides, by now we all know I am the queen of disappearing acts, trust me, sexy chocolate wasn't the first. I had broken the news to my mom, who was in complete denial as well, but because of different reasons, apparently, her actions, in my childhood, were what caused the dissociation in the first place. My pastor, who was also family, was confused and, also refused to hear the madness.

He wanted a second opinion, which I assured him, I had already done before coming to him. In his mind, it was surely the devil, I had opened-up a door to him and I was clearly possessed by demons that needed expulsion. Yeah, that didn't work go over well, that's a whole other story. I was eventually excluded from serving in the church and asked to leave, in as nice a way as possible.

I was still just as confused as I was at the beginning. I was not upset though, with all that had been happening to me, I needed to be somewhere else, I just had no clue where to go. My mom eventually began to understand but was adamant that God could heal even this issue, after all, it's what we believed, there was no reason to doubt that now. It somehow gave me a sense of hope that I desperately needed at the time.

I needed to come to terms with my diagnosis, but I still had so many questions... Why did God allow me to be burdened with this? What was the purpose, everything had a purpose, right? What was I supposed to do? I remember, one time, going to my mother's house and staying there for about two weeks. She finally asked me why was I there, when I had a place of my own.

She realized that I was too scared to go home, and she was right, she prayed for me, then politely kick me out, what a mom. But, she was right, I need to face my life, as it was now.

I had still been seeing the other therapist, it had been a year by now. A lot had changed. I had taken care and custody of my troubled, teenaged goddaughter, who was way more than I had bargained for because she came with a myriad of problems of her own. I had also found out the guy I was seeing for years was cheating on me, again, during that whole year that I had taken him back. SMH. And what's sad is he was still the main person who was there for me through all this craziness.

He was my main support, at times, my only support, now what? On a good note, I had found an awesome church and pastor, I was not misplacing my car anymore, and I had not had any spells during driving. I was, however, still losing track of time and my keys on a regular.

"One day at a time, trust God," I told myself constantly. I felt a nervous breakdown on the way.

Welcome to my crazy life

I guess it's only fair that I digress, yet again. To help you understand this crazy thing, I call my life now, you need to understand what DID really does to your life. Dissociative Identity Disorder is something that is brought on by trauma as a child. It is not hereditary, like other mental health disorders. When a trauma happens to a child, and they cannot mentally deal, they turn off, disconnect, or dissociate from the situation to keep themselves from having to deal with it, mainly out of fear.

When this happens, the mind creates an alternate person that takes on the life happenings at that moment and becomes a part of that person, yet separate. Once it happens the first time, the brain understands this as the new defense mechanism, and any trauma after that causes the same thing to happen. New trauma, new split from the "Core/Main" person. (Side note disclaimer: I'm no therapist, but this is the only way I know how to explain it.)

It's the reason I forget (conversations, things, people). The reason I lose track of time. The reason I have insomnia, because, if I'm sleeping, someone is up. It affects how I socialize, how I relate and adapt to people and surroundings, how I cope with circumstances that arise. For example, If I am in a heated debate with my man, and I feel anxious. Nine times out of ten, the conversation will be finished by an alternate personality.

Depending on the conversation, my level of anxiety or anger, and how aggressive the conversation, these things all determine who will finish the interaction. But the kicker is, most times I won't always know what happened, or what was said after the switch, and may not come right back out straight away. Which leads to other issues. Let's just say a relationship with me, can be quite interesting and takes a special kind of someone.

Coming to Grip

My therapist had by then introduced me to my "alternate personalities." Since I had not had the best response from my family members, I decided not to tell anyone else in my family and turned to my friends, who seemed to be way more understanding, even though they themselves were confused. They were supportive, and that's all I could ask for at the time.

Some of them needed to know and understand, how they can tell the difference between the "other ME's." While some, didn't care about the logistics, they just understood, one body means they are all me in some way, and that was good enough. One friend offered advice, which at first, I resented because I felt, I was at that pivotal point of accepting my diagnosis; we were eating at our favorite Thai restaurant, and she said:

"You are not your diagnosis. Do not take hold and claim this as who you are. This should never become your norm."

Huh? What was she talking about, I thought. This was my life, it is my norm. I wanted to get defensive, but I knew she had never steered me wrong before and went home to pray on it, for clarity. I needed to know what my life was, if it was not what it had become. Who was I now, if not defined by this? The old me, pre-diagnosed, seemed so far away.

The stress was starting to wear down on me and I still was having normal life happening as well. So again, I ran from life, another disappearing act. I packed, got in my car, and my little dog and I were on the road, not having a clue where I was going. I needed to get away from where I was and didn't want anyone to know.

After a seven-hour drive, I ended up at my aunt's house in New Jersey. If you knew her, you would know, that was a No, No! She's the type that will not open the door and leave you outside banging. When she heard, it was me, surprisingly she opened it. Tears in my eyes and dog in my arms, she stepped back and let us in, saying,

"And he better not urinate on my floor!"

She was the one person, since childhood who I always seemed to have a special connection with to talk about things. Especially the things I didn't want people to know. I think it was because I knew she was like me, at times strong, but at times weighed down by life, however, we always managed to get through. I knew she would help me and I knew she would never tell. I stayed there for three days, in silence, in the dark basement apartment. Finally, she came down on day four and said:

"Let's go! You've been down here long enough alone, what's going on with you?"

We ate some Italian food and sipped on some wine, I poured out my heart and told her my story. She never said a word. I cried, I stopped, and then cried some more. When it was all said, and done, she had given me the courage to go home and face my life again. My seven-hour drive home seemed way shorter than the long drive I had taken a few days before.

THE READY WOMAN

My life was flipped upside down. And this Jersey girl who was always strong and knew who she was, found out she was not as strong as she thought, and became as lost as a ship at sea. But I held on to God and my circle of friends, and family that was there for me. I finally figured out who I was, and it was not a woman tied to a diagnosis. I was not defined by this notion of hopelessness and Mental Illness.

I was not going to be the woman who stayed in a dead-end, emotionally abusive relationship because of a stale thought life, that says, "who would want a woman with my condition?" I dropped all the dead weight I could find relationships, job, responsibilities, whatever was negative and held me down.

I decided to give my life a makeover. I decided it was worth living and fighting for, that I was worth the effort. I went back to doing what I loved, working as a Nanny. I have since worked with some of the best agencies, and some high-profile clientele, one of them being Saudi Arabian Royalty.

I started a dog grooming and boarding business, which I successfully ran for over five years. I got to serve in my new church on their leadership team and loved it. I recently moved to a new state, for a new position with a family. I have met the most fantastic guy, who adores me, even with my diagnosis. We have a healthy relationship because God has done the best healing job on my heart! And I am now co-authoring this book!

What does this mean to you...

Being a Ready Woman is no easy task. It takes hard work, dedication, and most of all, self-evaluation. You should ask yourself and others the hard questions about you and respect the answers you receive. You must know that it demands a change in your life.

Everyone will not accept the change and stay around. And you should be ok with who you must leave behind. And trust, there will be someone.

Being a Ready Woman means, you can do the unthinkable and damn near impossible, once you make up your mind to do it. It means putting God first! It means setting goals and planning, and not just, living on the wind and a prayer. Getting someone to hold you accountable, and then being accountable to them. It means getting vision and then making it a priority.

I am a Ready Woman because I did these things and more because I am still moving forward and accomplishing. Because I choose to make a difference in others' lives as well. Because I choose to serve and give freely. I chose to overcome my fears.

You can be a Ready Woman, by doing the same. And by knowing that if you have a mental health illness or anything that keeps you in the same place, know that you can push forward. Never let anyone make you think you cannot be successful or useful. You are not average, by any means, we all have something unique about us. We all have PURPOSE!

About the Author

For over two decades, Kimberly Brown has supported career parents, by supervising, nurturing, guiding, and inspiring their children as a career nanny. Caring for minors ranging from infancy-teenagers. Brown works both as live-in and-out, as well as, on-call, and travel nanny capacities, all over the world.

Her mantra, *"It takes a village to raise a child, and I'm a village leader,"* is what she prides her work ethic around. Her career as a nanny began in 1996, and she later obtained her Professional Nanny Certification, in 2009. Working with the industries top placement agencies, helping train nannies, and being a member of the International Nanny Association, she has solidified her career as an Infant/Newborn Care Specialist.

Diversity is a strength she developed while working with children with special needs, multiples, or unique family circumstances. Kimberly Brown, also known as, Nanny Kim on the Go, has learned to empower parents and children alike, helping to sharpen their communication skills and pinpoint challenging areas to be transformed by her experience and wisdom.

Past and current clientele includes well-known television news anchors, philanthropists, millionaires, and The Saudi Royal Family. Ms. Brown, is the owner of Nanny Kim on the Go, an experienced Professional Nanny Training & Parent Consultant Agency, based in Northern New Jersey, offering supportive services to parents in the hiring and training process of qualified, attentive, and experienced nannies.

kimcbrown78@gmail.com
www.facebook.com/1NannyKimonthego/
www.instagram.com/allgodiva/

Dedication and Acknowledgements

I would like to dedicate my writing to my Grandmother, Lois Brown-Duncan, who although is deceased, has always been the reason I have pushed past trails and always persevere. She encouraged writing, education, and promoted individualism and freedom. I owe her everything.

I would like to share this moment with my close circle of family and friends, who no matter what, they were and are there for me, and helped me through my toughest period, sometimes without even knowing. My mother (Kim), Aunt's Adrienne, Crystal, Sharon, and Sylvia. Friends Nakita, Lesha, Marsha, Jennifer, Henricka, Sonya, Cynthia, Monica, Jacelyn, and Tequilla x2. And to My King, Shakim, who encouraged me to write something meaningful, helpful, and liberating. THANKS FOR ALWAYS BEING THERE, I TRULY LOVE YOU ALL.

Personal Notes:

_____

_____

_____

_____

_____

_____

_____

_____

Diary Entry 8
H.U.N.T.E.R.
By Marla Fowlkes

dear diary.

It's me Marla...   *June 9, 2009*

Hope. Until. Next. Triumph. Embraces.Restoration.

And then she was gone. My baby was dead. Her lifeless body lying in the hospital operating bed, with glassy eyes facing me in a still glare. I was devastated. How could this have happened? How could my 7.2 oz. baby not be alive? My husband Kevin stood there in disbelief with tears in his eyes. As he held me, I cried the ugliest and most heart-wrenching cry that only a grieving mother could.

The feeling of emptiness consumed me for the next six months. I was leaving the hospital without my child. Hunter Kemarri Fowlkes, whom I carried for eight months, was no more. I could not get that vision out of my head: Her lying there with her eyes open, not a single breath left in her tiny body.

The Journey Begins

At age 42, I was told at 12 weeks into my pregnancy that my baby's heart had a hole in it. The doctor relayed that as long as I made it to term, the baby would be okay. Sometimes the hole closes by itself and other times it requires surgery immediately after birth. I was thinking...

Good grief, now I am deemed high risk for two reasons: I'm over the age of 35, and my baby has a congenital disability. My mind started racing with the question: Will my baby be ok? What type of tests will I have to endure throughout the course of my pregnancy? Will I make it to full term? This was my first child. I finally decided to start a family and my baby has a birth defect. Great. The journey had just begun, but I had no idea what would transpire in the coming months. I changed my work schedule so that I could be off every other Monday for all of my bi-weekly OB/ GYN appointments.

Trimesters...

Because I was overweight and my blood pressure and glucose levels were borderline when I got pregnant, they monitored me closely. I was given a glucose meter and had to record my glucose readings daily. I was beginning to worry that the baby would make my problems worse. At 15 weeks, I had to get tested to see if the baby had Trisomy 21 which causes Down Syndrome. What the hell is an amniocentesis? I was nervous. I wasn't sure if I wanted prenatal testing. The length of the needle made it scarier! If my baby had it, was I going to terminate the pregnancy? Do I want to raise a child with special needs?

Will I have adequate resources? Kevin and I decided that it would be best to know ahead of time. If the baby had it, we agreed that we would do our research and would raise a child with special needs. Well, the test results came back positive. Wow. The first thing you do is question: Why me? Why does my baby have three copies of the chromosome 21 instead of two? Was I even up for this type of challenge? In any event, we participated in the initial genetic counseling to learn about the abnormality. In my mind, I kept wondering: Was it something wrong with me that caused it? After learning about abnormal cell division, I realized there was nothing I could have done to prevent it. I had to accept it. There was no way of knowing how severe the syndrome would be until the baby was born and started developing. I just kept praying. Technology is amazing. They can tell so early if things are wrong with the embryo or fetus. In a way, I was grateful. There would be no surprises.

Researching Trisomy 21, I realized that the abnormality caused the hole in the heart as well. Now, I was mentally dealing with two issues upon my baby's arrival: Surgery and a form of retardation. It takes strength to raise a child with special needs. We shall see.

Surprisingly, I had a great pregnancy. I worked all the way up to my eighth month. I rarely got morning sickness. Every day around 3 p.m. I would get nauseated, but cold beverages relieved it. The worst symptom I had was gagging every morning when I brushed my teeth. That was crazy! The struggle was real with such a simple hygiene task. I ate just about everything. My biggest craving was McDonald's Big Mac. I wasn't sure if it was the special sauce or what, but my husband was going to McDonald's almost once a week. Nothing made me sick except the smell of fresh mulch. I remember holding my breath as I left work in early Spring. I almost ran to my car to turn on the air conditioning, so I wouldn't throw up in the parking lot. Other than that, I was doing good. I could attend President Obama's inauguration, I stood on my feet for hours. It was incredible but freezing. I even participated in a conference in Washington, DC days before I went into labor.

I was eight months pregnant, and my situation started going downhill. During a routine checkup, my doctor relayed that my pressure was high. She kept taking readings, but it would not go down. Then she made me lay on my left side for a while and retook my pressure. I was thinking... I feel fine. Why is my pressure high? She told me I could be developing preeclampsia, so they had to watch me overnight to see if I was spilling ketones and protein in my urine. I was afraid. Reality finally hit me! I'm going to push this mini human being out of my vagina.

I could have sworn that anyone who came into my room could hear my heart beating. The heartbeat was strong and loud to me. I don't think I slept at all that night. The next morning came, and the doctor gave me the bad news. I had developed preeclampsia, so I would be in the hospital until delivery.

Three days in, they are continuing to check glucose levels. The doctor orders me a shot of insulin. Here we go. Things are worsening. Mentally, I was not doing well. I just wanted it to be over. I was so over all the probing, sticking, poking and needles. Days before my delivery, they checked me to see if my water broke. Kevin sat with me daily trying not to look worried. He wanted me to feel better, but it was nothing he could do but wait it out.

Labor and Delivery

Suddenly, all this water started gushing down my leg. I didn't think anything of it since my body was doing what it wanted to at that point. I felt like I had heartburn, so I called the nurse, and she brought me some Gas X tablets. The heartburn didn't get better, so I thought... am I in labor? Kevin had just left. I was trying to figure things out. I didn't know how labor was supposed to feel. I went to get out of the bed, and a cramp hit me so hard it brought me to my knees. I hit the panic button and told the nurse I was cramping. The doctor came to the room, she said:

"It's time. I've watched this show long enough from the monitor."

I was like ... "What... my husband just left." I called him back as they were wheeling me to the delivery room. I kept thinking these labor pains are going to kick my ass. I'll never make it through the delivery.

As Kevin rubbed my back and kept a cool compress on my head, the doctor told me I could get an epidural when it was time. More probing, I was about to lose it! There was a team of doctors surrounding the bed. Everyone was giving me direction and calling my name. All of sudden I was in the midst of my first panic attack. I remember yelling and telling everyone to leave me alone. I just wanted to go through the pain alone.

I no longer wanted my vitals checked, and the beeping of the monitor was driving me nuts! The probing and sticking were too much. The doctor came in and told Kevin she would give me something to calm me down. I watched her put something in my IV. I started fading fast. I dozed off only to wake up only by contractions.

It was finally time for the epidural. Kev held me down as they placed five capsules in my back.

I was in labor for six hours. I was so out of it, and I could barely push. The doctor had to watch the monitor to tell when I was having a contraction. Kevin would wake me up out of my nod to tell me to push. This ritual went on for the whole delivery. I was finally able to push the head out. All of sudden, I looked up and saw a panic look on the doctor's face. Apparently, my muscles had clamped down on the baby's neck. She had to act quickly. The doctor proceeded to give me a third-degree episiotomy. In that instant, I wish I had opted for a cesarean. All I could hear was Kevin saying...

"You have to fix that. I was very fond of that."

Hunter Kemarri Fowlkes was born at 6:08 am on May 29, 2009. I watched them wipe her off, swaddle her and carry her out of the room. She was gorgeous! A high yellow baby with straight, cold black hair.

I was still lying on the table at 7:10 a.m. as they stitched me up. I was in pain everywhere in my body. The doctor asked the anesthesiologist to administer more pain meds, but he relayed he couldn't give me anything else that could numb the rectum. I could feel the needle go in each time the doctor made a stitch. She was pulling the stitches tight like she was sewing buttons on a wool coat. Tears flowed from my eyes, but the pain took my breath. I could not make a sound. I laid on the bed like a bloody piece of meat. My mind racing-- my vagina, and rectum would be forever damaged goods.

They finally wheeled me to recovery and placed compression on my legs to help squeeze out all the fluid. I still had the catheter in place. I was a hot mess! My body had been through tremendous trauma. How can women keep having kids? They must be nuts! I lay there in bed with my ass on a block of ice. My mom and sister came to see me. They looked relieved. I looked at the monitor, and I saw a 50 as the top number of my blood pressure reading. Was my pressure that low? OMG! My mother looked worried, and the doctor put something in the IV to bring my pressure up.

At 10:00 a.m., my Pastor was sitting in the guest chair asking me if I wanted to have another one. I told him it was too early for jokes. I was bedridden, so I couldn't see her in NICU. Kevin went to see her and reported that she was the biggest thing in NICU. We laughed and breathed a sigh of relief. The next morning, they removed the catheter and asked me to attempt to urinate on my own. I walked gingerly to the bathroom and peed on a slant. At least it still worked. I made it back to the bed and laid there. I felt like shit.

The pediatric cardiologist reported that Hunter was doing OK, but he would still have to do the surgery. She didn't need it immediately. He would do the surgery in 11 days. I was released three days after delivery. I was home trying to make sense of what happened. My body was hurting. I used the 11 days to rest and pump breast milk. Every day I went to the hospital to visit my baby. I had my baby shower a week after I got home since I had her a month early. Hunter, my little girl, had so many gifts including a leopard and pink spa bathrobe. I couldn't wait to bring her home.

The Surgery

On the 11th day, Hunter had surgery. We kissed her and prayed over her before they wheeled her into surgery not knowing that was the last time we would ever see our baby alive. Kevin and I stayed at the hospital until she had made it out of surgery. Once she was stable, we left to go home to get more clothes since we had decided we would spend the night at the hospital.

Before we could get back to the hospital, they called us and asked how soon we could get back. They relayed they had to code her and were able to bring her back. We got back to the hospital in record time. Now, at the hospital, we were super worried, but she was still alive. The doctor comes to the waiting room to tell us she went into cardiac arrest a second time, but they could not bring her back. They felt that she had been on the bypass machine too long as an infant, but it was necessary to repair the heart. It was all for nothing.

The Aftermath

How am I going to get through this? I was hysterical. The coming days would be challenging. Kevin was strong for me but for how long? I could not get it together...unable to function...unable to think. I could not eat. That was the fastest weight loss ever. I had lost 70 lbs. in three months. Half of that was fluid but still fast nonetheless. How was I going to sit through the funeral director and church meetings, memorial service, and burial? Death feels final. I cried every single night for I don't know how long. Kev and I talked to Pastor and quickly realized we could not handle a funeral with the body in a small casket at the church.

We had a memorial service for our Hunter instead. It was beautiful. The church had done an excellent job creating the memorial. There wasn't an empty seat in the house. Everything was perfect...even down to my pink outfit which I haven't worn since the service. How am I going to bury my baby? I could not. I would not. Kevin told the funeral director that he would carry his baby in his truck and bury her. I couldn't go. The grief was too much for me. The day of the burial I went to the funeral home after Kevin picked out her outfit. She had begun to swell a little. I could barely look at the lifeless body as she laid in the tiny casket at the funeral home.

I glanced at her but noticed everything. Her eyes were closed, and she had on a top that said Daddy's little girl. I almost sprinted out of the room, and Kevin and the funeral director took her to the burial ground.

Everything was difficult. I couldn't remember things. When I couldn't remember where I lived, I knew I needed therapy. I contacted my health care provider and they gave me a referral to see a psychiatrist to make sure I was not depressed. I was not depressed. I was just grieving the loss of my daughter. My mind was gone. I zoned out a lot. I was unable to work. I remember having to take Tylenol PM just to sleep. I couldn't keep up with my keys. I was forcing myself to eat just a little bit. I met the psychiatrist. That turned out to be a bad experience.

She was incredibly insensitive and looked like she was about 30 years old. She recommended I go back to work to try to jump back into the swing of things. I looked her in her face and told her I couldn't even remember where I lived. How in the hell am I going to work? She then suggested I see a therapist.

I met with the therapist who really helped me sort things out in my own time. She realized that it will take time to heal both mentally and physically from my loss. Things slowly started to improve. Thank goodness for job benefits. I had AFLAC that provided an income once my leave ran out. I joined the Voluntary Leave Transfer Program and employees were able to donate hours to me. I never missed a paycheck. I was advanced sick leave to cover a period of time as well.

My baby girl was gone. I would never get to breastfeed her or rock her to sleep or tell her stories or watch her eat goodies. Speaking of goodies...It was so funny because, during those 11 days leading up to her surgery, I would talk about all the good food her and I would eat or have eaten. As I whispered those things, she would never open her eyes. She would just lick her lips—every time. It was the cutest thing! Kevin would tell me she was going to be greedy like her mother. At that moment, my mind started wandering. I was thinking about all that stored breast milk I pumped that I had to throw away. We were approaching summer. The first two weeks of June was not good. Kevin's birthday was overshadowed by Hunter's death. She passed away one minute before his birthday.

How am I going to get through all these special days? May and June had delivered both joy and sorrow. Until this day it is still bittersweet. My birthday and my sister's birthday are in May. Mother's Day is in May. My wedding anniversary is in May. June is not much better with Kevin's birthday being so close to Hunter's death. Father's Day is a week after his birthday. It was hard to keep it together while everyone was celebrating Mother's Day. Was I even a mother with nothing to show for it? I would often ask myself that question. My mom and sister told me from the beginning that I will always be a mother even though Hunter was my angel who touched down just for a minute.

I just took each day as it came. I cried on all of them for the first three years. Family and friends helped me get through it. They were there for me...there for us. My church family was the best! They came over every day for weeks just to sit with me, run errands, clean up, tire me out, etc. They even picked shells out of crabmeat for me. And... I had more roasted chickens than I knew what to do with. Even though I saw them weekly, I was not ready to step foot back in the church. I just wasn't ready. I was still questioning God. I wasn't willing to hear the dreaded question... "Are you going to try again?" I stayed prayed up though. Every day I asked God to give me the strength I needed to get back on my feet...mentally, physically and spiritually.

It was indeed a steep road. Therapy helped me. The therapist told me I would not have to decide right away about getting pregnant again. At first, I thought...Why not? I'm already freaking 42. Time was not on my side. However, each session she reminded me of how my life would dictate whether or not I would try again. She was right. Each day got a little easier for me.

However, Kevin was beginning to weaken. He had been strong for me in the beginning, and he needed to be. Now, it was his time to grieve finally. He also felt a particular kind of way since all the emphasis and empathy had been on me. It was understandable, but he had experienced a loss as well. It was a difficult time in our marriage. We had to hold each other up.

We would cry when we watched certain movies or if we saw babies. It was crazy. Only time would heal us.

Getting Back to Normal

Things continued to improve. My body was slowly healing. And... boy was it slow! My glucose levels returned to normal. The excess fluid was gone. I dropped some pounds. My blood pressure improved, but it never returned to normal without medication. I had experienced extreme constipation and was afraid to eat anything. In any event, I made all my follow-up appointments to the doctor. Months later, I remember going back to OB/GYN and my doctor telling me I had healed nicely. She told me I was healthier enough to try again. I just smiled but was thinking... *not right now doc.*

I finally went back to work and slowly eased back into my workload. Everyone was happy to see I was doing better. This whole ordeal was a process. Hunter's social security card and health insurance card came in the mail. I remember laying both on the table next to her death certificate. In addition, Kev and I had attended the memorial program given by the hospital's pediatric unit. It was a lovely ceremony...remembering all the children and babies who were no longer with us.

When things happen such as this, you always think of something you could have done differently. If I had to do it over again, I would have gotten healthier before my pregnancy. I would have gotten pregnant ten years prior. Would that have changed the outcome? Maybe. But...those were the life cards that were dealt to me. I told God, I tried it, and it did not work.

Kevin and I discussed the idea of trying again. He was open to whatever I wanted to do. He was alright with it if I wanted to try again. He was also fine with it if I chose not to. He already had children from a previous marriage. The day had come when I decided I did not want to try again. I felt like my life had dictated what I needed to do.

THE READY WOMAN

We all possess strength, but you don't know how strong you are until you have to experience something tragic. You have to be strong in your faith knowing that somehow it will all work out. Am I stronger because of it? Absolutely! I have more of an appreciation for life after the death of my Hunter. Life is precious, and it can be over in an instant.

As a Management Analyst, I run a professional mentoring program for approximately 6,000 employees. I believe you can always learn from someone else. We didn't come into this world knowing everything, and we won't be leaving this world knowing everything. However, we will be departing much wiser through trials and tribulations and learning from those who paved the way for us. To God be the Glory!

Today, I help women become a healthier more confident person. I show them how to put themselves first and to embrace who they are no matter her size. We are all beautiful! As Brand Ambassador for Smooches Models DMV- Baltimore, I encourage women to build their confidence and embrace a positive body image. Life will beat you down if you let it, but you must brush yourself off and get back up. That is one reason I promote health and wellness, especially in the curvy community. We all have our level of being fit, but you must start somewhere. Find something you like and stick with it.

I wrote my story to inspire women, and hopefully, I was able to provide that light at the end of the tunnel. What's your takeaway? When you are going through life's toughest challenge, create a plan of action:

1. Evaluate the situation: Who is being harmed? Is professional assistance required? Who else is being affected? Are there available resources? What's the worst-case scenario?

2. Find at least one person you can trust. At some point, you may need to confide in that person.

3. Create a positive circle. Befriend those women who can provide resources, comfort and time. You will need them at some point. Distant yourself from those who slowly suck the life from you with their drama.

4. Pray daily. Prayer and meditation will help you center yourself and think more clearly about the situation.

5. Trust your gut. Women do possess a sixth sense. Intuition is so powerful and doesn't ignore the feeling.

Whatever your challenge, believe you will get through it. Enjoy those precious moments of this thing called life. We create life. Embrace that and become the strong, beautiful person, called the woman. My name is Marla Fowlkes, and I am a Ready Woman!

About the Author

Marla Fowlkes, The Curvy Evolutionist Smooches Brand Ambassador DMV- Baltimore & plus size model is an active Baltimorean and a woman of God who enjoys life to the fullest. She can motivate and engage the most unyielding introvert. Marla is a Management Analyst for the Centers for Medicare and Medicaid Services (CMS) where she manages the CMS Mentoring Program for approximately 6,000 employees and serves as a Contracting Officer's Representative in the CMS Leadership Institute for the Division of Talent Development. At CMS, Marla also facilitates the bi-weekly New Employee Orientation sessions where she conducts presentations for all new employees.

As Smooches Brand Ambassador and Plus Size Model for the Smooches Movement in the DMV-Baltimore Metropolitan Area, Marla empowers women in the "curvy" community. She shows women how to build confidence and put themselves first. Marla believes when women realize that they are beautiful, it becomes the most important step in loving themselves. Marla is also an Independent Beauty Consultant for Mary Kay Cosmetics. She uses her products and services to enhance the lives of women and to empower them financially as well.

In addition, Marla is an active Toastmaster and served as Vice President of Membership for CMS Toastmasters Club #8470 for over three years. As a confidence builder, Marla encourages women to become comfortable talking to a crowd as well as one-on-one settings. It doesn't stop there. Marla hosts and promotes large events for local DJs and promoters in the Baltimore area.

Marla helps others achieve a healthier "curvy and fit" lifestyle through coaching and demonstrates how a balanced healthier lifestyle can benefit them in all areas of their lives. With her own testimony, Marla has taught women to make health a priority. Healthy is the new sexy!

If you are in the Baltimore-Washington Metropolitan area, you may catch Marla at speaking engagements, campaigns, radio shows, pageants, fashion shows, vending opportunities, empowerment conferences, showcases, ministry/community projects, expos, private parties, fitness/wellness events and more.

When Marla is not working at CMS and/or helping others achieve a healthier lifestyle, she enjoys her "chill time" with her loving husband Kevin Fowlkes. Marla works it out on the dance floor in her Zumba, Cize Live, Kangoo Jump, and Hot Hula classes three-four days a week! She also enjoys line dancing, cruises, fine dining, networking and a good horror movie.

If you are looking to make that change to a healthier more confident you, contact Marla using the following:

www.curvyevolutionist.com

www.marykay.com/mfowlkes

www.facebook.com/marla.fowlkes

www.instagram.com/Felicity_Fowlkes

Dedication and Acknowledgements

I dedicate this book collaboration to my beautiful daughter Hunter Kemarri Fowlkes. You touched down from Heaven for just a moment. A precious life...a piece of me...a fragile face of innocence... my Hunter. You will always live in my heart. Until we meet again... I want you to know that Mommy will always love you! *#HUNTER*

I also dedicate this book collaboration to the women who have ever experienced the loss of her child. It is a pain like no other. The pain never goes away. It just becomes easier to bear. Therefore, know that you will get through it with prayer and support from family and friends. Know that you don't have to go through it alone. Embrace those helping hands and your journey to restoration will be inevitable.

I would like to thank my loving husband Kevin Darnell Fowlkes. He has been my rock through the years through this traumatic loss. While the focus tends to be on the mother when a child dies, the father must remain strong to take care of the arrangements if you will. He is the pillar. I was not able to witness my daughter's burial. My husband drove her in his truck and carried the small casket all the way to burial site to the plot where he will be buried as well. I could never have mustered up enough strength to do such a thing. I will always love him for that. We had many sleepless nights where we held each other and cried. To my Puddin...I love you.

I would also like to thank my family and friends for just being there for me. I needed every one of you. Special thanks to my mother Ellen Cosby, my sister Kara Williams, and my nephew Ivory Williams, Jr.—we all mourned "Hunter." I love you. Special thanks to Pastor Franklin Lance, D. Min. and my MLBC family. What a blessing! Pastor... I still don't know how you got to the hospital so fast. From the tons of cards and well wishes I received to the beautiful memorial service, my church family came through without hesitation. I thank you all!

And... last but not least to my *"bestie"* Kimberly France-Presco. You will always be my "ride or die." We have been through so much together. I cannot thank you enough for all the 28+ years of friendship. Thank you for being you. I love me some Kimmy!

Personal Notes:

_____

_____

_____

_____

_____

_____

_____

_____

_____

_____

_____

_____

_____

_____

Diary Entry 9
In My Father's House
By Syrita Lindsey

dear diary

It's me Syrita...   *April 18, 2010*

I Gotta Pee

I awaken in the emergency room, lying in a hospital bed. When I regained my focus, there were a couple of cops in the room appearing to be standing on guard. I scanned the remains of the room and realized that they were perhaps there for me? What the what? Suddenly, I had to pee. It was like the movies—only I was the villain, captured in my sleep.

My good nursing friend was at my bedside. She had seen the horrific car wreck on television and immediately came to my bedside. God sent her to see about me. I could hear my family outside my door. What the freak?

"I gotta pee. I got to pee now and badly!" My voice was hoarse and unsteady. I spoke to the ER nurse.

"Okay" replied the nurse.

"Hum, we are going to need a sample of her urine," interjected this tall, dark and well-defined cop.

"Oh, HELL and Oh, No, do you have a warrant for the sample, Mr. Officer?" My girl said in her "You betta try that shit on someone who doesn't know" voice.

"Slam Dunk, my girl! Damn, that was good thinking because I did not think of that."

"Yeah, do you have a warrant?" The ER nurse chimed in with the same question. Well, look here. 'Get'em girls,' I thought.

"Hold on, Nurse Betty." My girl said while side eyeing her but maintaining her focus on her new prey.

My girl turned to me and said, "You betta piss in your pants!" With a slight chuckle, "Don't mind if I do." Relief came, but the officer was pissed.

I vaguely remembered that my cousin pulled me out of the car. I kept asking anyone who would listen. "How bad did I fuck him up? How bad?" Referring to the truck I hit. As I approached the decline of the road, all I saw was a huge RAM truck. The impact from me running into him was sudden and swift. Our degrees of separation were zero. My head hit the front window shield.

My vision blurred, not from the consumption of alcohol, but from the copious amounts of blood that were gradually saturating my eyelids. One can liken it to the horror movie 'Carrie' when she was standing on stage drenched in pig's blood, only it was my own.

Brittany Needed Cash

"What do you mean, you want cash?" My voice escalating in response to her request. I knew that I should be firm on my "no" to my cousin.

I had just finished working 72 hours in one week as a Registered Nurse, and I had planned on going home and sleeping for the next day or so. Working night shift at the hospital had its benefits, but it is demanding on the mind, body, and spirit.

If I had only followed my gut and refused from the beginning perhaps, I would not be giving you an account of my situation. That is not true because this or worse was bound to happen to me.

It was my hairdresser, Cousin Brittany, on the line. Yes, I could afford to go to the shop, but she was having it rough and was my way to help her without-flat out giving her money. It was as if she set her alarm to my pay week.

"Rita, can I please do your hair today? I need to pay the electric bill." Brittany asked as I chirped the lock on my new Lexus RX300. I grinned at the '2Rita' on the plates. I was both arrogant and cocky, but I will come back to that later.

"Damn, Brittany, I am tired! It is eight o'clock in the morning, and I am just getting off. By the way, what are you doing up ANY-WAY?" Rolling my eyes and turning on the seat warmer. Yeah, it is April, but I liked my ass hot.

"Rita, come on, let me do your hair, huh?" she begged, "I need to keep the lights on."

"Fine, just come on." I reluctantly replied. Damn, I just wanted to go home, have a couple of glasses of wine, shower, and sleep – in that exact order.

I knew it was going to be an all-day process, so I stopped and picked some wine and food from the grocery store.

'Ding Dong.' Is that the doorbell, already? Crap, that was quick! If I did not know better, one would think she lived next door.

However, it was not the case because I moved out to Black Lick area of Columbus Ohio, a distance away from urban happenings. It was a part of my Black Woman's 'Arrival Package.' A brand new built home to match the brand-new Lexus, to match that brand-new money I was representing.

Cocky? Yes. arrogant? For sure. Self-Assured? Most def. Can I? Quit playing, you already know. Intelligent? Check my stats.

I openly considered myself the poster child of a Black Women pulling herself up by the bootstraps. On the other hand, so I thought. Understand I had narrowly escaped the tragedies of growing up in a dysfunctional home that riddled with drugs, alcohol, and domestic violence yet seasoned with enough love to sustain hope and faith for betterment. I cheated and sidestepped the stigma and woes of teen-age pregnancy by aborting my child when I was 14 without my parent's knowledge. I was determined not to become the statistic that I created at an early age.

"Girl, come on in." Opening the door now excited to see that she brought Alexandria, her daughter. Alexandria was as cute as morning dew of a sunflower. Saucy and full of life like her mother.

Opening my front door on that beautiful crisp April morning forever changed how doors would permanently close right before me.

We ate and drank while Brit braided my hair. Brit was very good at her trade, and it allowed me to stay cute and work long hours at the hospital.

"Cuz, I am going to need cash and not a check today," Brit said on the sly while packing her belongings.

"What do you mean, you want cash? Brit, you know I don't have any cash money." I bellowed.

I was tired and ready for bed. Instantly, my gut said, "don't give in...don't." Now, this is some shit because I always pay Brit with a check. Rarely, do I carry cash. Agitation and irritation overloaded my nervous system.

The phone abruptly interrupted my irritation. It was Chris, my man. I told him that I was about to go to the ATM for Brit. He insisted that I not go but pay her with a check. God gives us a warning before destruction we must have an ear to listen.

As we left, Alex said, "Aunt Rita, may I ride with you?"

"Sure, Sweat Pea," I responded even though I am her second cousin.

Now honestly, nothing happened on a human level that would have deterred Alex from climbing into my Lexus. God interceded on Alex's course and started me on a new one.

I failed to buckle up for what would be a ride of a lifetime. Turned up my favorite theme song "I Want It All" by Warren G, and popped the top of the sunroof.

The Crash

Before the car accident, I did not believe I was an alcoholic. I knew that it was rampant in my family tree, however, I assumed since I worked hard I could play hard and play included the consumption of alcohol. On countless occasions, I have driven under the influence of alcohol. I never considered the impact or harm that my drinking caused others. I fully participated on a regular basis in a selfish and self-centered act.

The blackouts I experienced were only actualized the next day when friends explained my behavior from the night before. I would laugh or just dismiss the stories, but I was embarrassed and ashamed of the event reporting.

Now I had seriously injured another human. I had lived a life of service to others, but my actions had negatively affected another being. I caused harm to perfect strangers. No words, thoughts, or drink could disturb or distort the reality that I created. If in fact, I did not deem myself an alcoholic before the proof was somewhere in this very hospital in surgery.

Mr. Golden, the victim of my drinking and driving, will forever remember me because he will never walk the same. When the cold of winter brisk by his leg, he will recount my name.

When arthritis knocks at his bones with pain, he will forever remember me. No amount of amends can repair Mr. Golden's leg but in the following years to come his pain and suffering will forever direct my conscious and actions.

I drank with a purpose following the accident. I slowly slipped into a depressive state. The irony is that alcohol is a depressant, so I was adding a depressant to my depression. It became hard living with myself knowing that I truly hurt someone. No longer did I feel secure. No longer did I even feel human. I felt less than, and undeserving.

I felt alone. Consuming alcohol and lying awake in a darkened space seemingly void of life. Chris and my family snatched me from slipping into the abyss. God helps us even when we know we are not deserving of such mercy and grace. With time, I grew a little stronger and decided to fulfill a goal of mine and join the Air Force as a Registered Nurse (what I know today it is called a geographical move only you still take the problem with you).

Just as I was about to enlist, I get a certified letter. You know the type that looks like it is of grave importance.

"The prosecutor's office?" I mumbled. I open the letter...

"NO SHIT!" I screamed, my two dogs look up at me like hold that down we are trying to sleep!

Nine Felony Counts

What kind of shit? Nine Felony counts? Nine. Did I see NINE? Yep, N-I-N-E, don't get illiterate now! I flipped the envelope over to look again. The mail addressed to me. My legs gave way. I cried. Rolled over and cried some more. Total disbelief.

"It was a FREAKING car accident! I did not kill anyone." I exclaimed to the only ears available to hear...the walls. They had served me papers almost one year to date of the accident.

My life hastily went into a downward spiral. Before my first trial (hold on there was two), I would case the appointed judge's courtroom. I wanted to see the setup. I wanted to understand the justice or injustice I had to endure.

The judge was a black man. He seemed to be fair. Moreover, I felt a little at ease because it was the first time I had been in trouble so maybe I would get a fair trial. Wrong.

I Drank My Way Through the Trial

During the trial, my family showed up every day. Especially my father. He was my rock. He would pick me up every day during my trial proceedings, and we rode with a 20 oz. of Budweiser in the cup holder (it was not mine). He supported me. My father consoled me amid my anxiety. My dad required that I walk as confidently as he raised me with my head up and shoulders back.

Every day I would come home and drink. I tried to drown out the sadness. Drink away my depression and oppress the reality of my situation. Alcohol was no longer for fun it became a necessity to function. So, I came to believe.

On one occasion, my lawyer stepped to me. Close. Closer than the invisible bubble, we offer each other as humans. He sniffed me.

"Rita, have you been drinking?" he commanded. He was tall and somewhat a thick man in comparison to my new size ten body frame.

"I did very early this morning." I sheepishly replied as if he was my father.

"You have got to be fucking kidding! You mean you can't stop drinking long enough for us to fight for you?" he exclaimed in a fury.

He grabbed my 7-up bottle and slammed it into the trash. He turned to walk away then paused pointed his stern finger at the near-by fountain and hoarsely whispered, "If you get thirsty Rita, drink from that fucking water fountain. That one only, get it?"

"Yes, sir," I mumbled one octave above a whisper.

"You thirsty?" he demanded.

"No sir" I stammered with my eyes cast down.

He walked away talking to himself.

What I know today, is that it was the insanity from the disease of alcoholism. No sane person standing trial for drinking and driving would possibly consume alcohol while seated one chair from the bailiff who is sitting next to the court recorder who elbows touch the judges while typing! Insanity. Utterly insane.

The VERDICT

As if from a scene in the TV series, 'Law and Order,' the decision from the judge announced I am found guilty four out of nine counts. I was knocked for six after the ringing in my ears ceased but now the kicker... After the judge read the verdict, the prosecutor stood up and demanded a retrial for the remaining five counts.

If thoughts could kill, my next trial would be for murdering the prosecutor. Before the second trial, I had unofficially lost my home (rented it to low income). My Cadillac SRX (still vain) repossessed. I had been filling gallons of water from the local pond to flush the toilet. Chris had moved out, and I all had left were two dogs who eventually ran away (sad but true).

The second trial was completely different. Mr. Golden walked into the courtroom and winked at me. I thought he has me on tape drinking (part of my pretrial condition was to abstain from alcohol)! On recess, he walked right up to me. "Can we talk?" he asked while smiling. It made me nervous. Too many CSI television episodes were running through my head.

"Um, I was getting ready to smoke," I replied hoping that would deter him from his mission. My immediate thought was he was going to kill me on the ride down or out in the courthouse yard (stop judging it was how I felt).

"Okay, I don't smoke, but I will go with you." he merrily stated.

I looked at my father like you just going to let this man gun me down without a fight? His nonverbal reply girl, hurry back before recess is over. Isn't this about a you know-what? Damn.

When outside, Mr. Golden turned with his semi-unsteady gait (I should tell you that he has a permanent pin now, thanks to me).

"I forgive you." It was the most humbling words ever spoken to me in this lifetime. His approach was gentle and sincere.

Tears surged from the gushing and tumultuous river of my soul. It was as if the dam had given way. I just sobbed. I grabbed him, almost knocking him over. No words, the tears had numbed my vocal chords. Then a whisper erupted.

"I love you and never meant to cause you the pain and suffering that you have endured, please forgive me."

God creates situations of joy that shows us that He always has our back. The forgiveness of a stranger whom I had harmed mentally, physically and emotionally forgave me before I could ask. We talked and shared. God lifted burdened from the both of us. Mr. Golden had forgiven me, God forgave me long ago, but a process of forgiving myself truly had yet to begin.

I was found not guilty of the remaining five felony counts! God creates situations and miracles that are unmistakably and undeniably, His work. No prosecutor or judge can overturn God's verdict.

As part of my punishment, the judge sentenced me to 31 days in the county jail. I hear you... not a lot of time. Nevertheless, I beg to differ; it was more than enough for me! The judge expanded the sentence to cover the holidays. I spent July 4th to President's day in February, which almost spanned over one year. He also placed me on probation and mandatory alcohol treatment. What came in the form of punishment was God's intent for the development of a relationship with Him and the discovery of true self.

Surprise, yet another letter in the mail. Now my RN license was in jeopardy due to the felony convictions. The result was that I had a mandatory suspension of one year and had to sign a consent agreement with the State Board of Nursing with many conditions including calling seven days a week to an automatized random drug screen selector.

The Conviction Aftermath

I went through two trials, I was homeless (if you are over 21 and staying with others you are in this group my friend), no car, have a felony conviction, RN licenses suspend, low self-worth, cannot stop drinking and so now what? The greatest loss was losing me. I tried to hold on to the idea of *"me."* What I later realized is that God was in the process of reconstructing me. I was stripped of everything to get my life in order and to surrender my life to Gods goodness for me fully.

I would like to say that after the second trial I refrained from alcohol, that my belief in God divinely removed the taste and affinity to alcohol from my desires.

I changed my talks with God from that day forward. No longer did I pray to get out of trouble. I prayed for the strength to change. I prayed for the courage to stand again. I prayed for restoration of self-worth. I prayed for a purpose. I prayed for willingness and ability to learn to forgive myself daily.

Everything Has a Purpose

The greatest loss was the loss of self. I was ready to fight. I was willing to stand. I had one more in me. However, I realized I could not do it alone. It was as if God heard the bellowing of my cry.

Initially, I went to outpatient treatment. Again, answering the questions and participating, as a health professional was a breeze. I was merely going through the motions. Until that summer day, I was getting off the COTA city bus following my outpatient treatment for alcohol. I would stop at Kroger's Grocery Store to pick up a box of wine. Being in rehab outpatient and hearing the stories often made me "thirsty" after treatment.

I had to finish the wine before reaching my brother's house because his condition to me staying was no alcohol consumption. The sun was shining, and I could feel the rays kissing my ebony skin. I enjoyed the sun. I was just walking and sipping, sipping and walking. The interruption came with a phone call, and I had to answer – it was my counselor.

"Hello?" I answered trying to use my most professional voice to con ceal the fact I have been drinking.

"Pack your bags; you're going back to jail!" she demanded with all earnestness.

"Hey, that is a sick joke," I said while scanning my surrounding and draining the remaining of the box. If I were going, at least I would be relaxed.

"No goofy girl, I got you a spot as the inpatient for rehab." I could just see her skinning and be grinning as if she just solved my issue (unknown to me, she had). "What?" I almost choked on the Chardonnay and sounding professional went straight out the door. So off to rehab inpatient. I can do these two weeks. Then I became excited. I can learn the tools necessary to stay sober in two weeks, get a job, kick the renters out of my house and all will be restored.

After one month in rehab inpatient, another counselor suggested I go to an all women rehab center to live for six months.

"No way. I ain't got that to do!" I exclaimed (when in rehab talk like you are in rehab) while he sat in his chair smiling. Honestly, nothing was funny.

"And what do you have to do? Huh? Let me guess, go to work? Go home? Go back to school? What, Rita? Anything?" Mr. Scott contorted never looking up from his paperwork. Ain't he it?

He was correct. I had nothing. I had reached rock bottom. I was depleted of resources and needed a helping hand. I had the desire to stay sober.

Rehabilitation Created a Beautiful Butterfly

I began to dig in. I am a woman of strong will, strength, and determination. We slowly started focusing on myself. I became hungry for a relationship with a Power Greater than myself whom I call God and ways to self-improvement. I sought out help from my church, family and a couple of friends that remained tried and true. My mother never left my side.

In rehab, the women loved me until I could love myself surrounded me. They provided tools and coping practices to implement in my life. I took the cotton out of my ears and placed it into my mouth. I became a sponge. I wanted what they had to offer.

The restoration of my self-worth and self-esteem was rebirthed. The pure essences of empowerment became my reality. I was hunger again to live life. I had something to offer. Most importantly, we could uncover the dirt and filth that I felt about myself and rediscovered–self! We chipped away the stones, and my soul released unto me. No words to describe the new birth.

While in treatment I had the privilege to return and finish my graduate studies. What an amazing feeling to look out and see about 60 of my people cheering me on as I receive a Master of Business Administration! That is God and action.

I also received my RN license back (with conditions) one year to the date of my suspension. That is the God in me in action. I stayed in treatment for one and one-half years. I enjoyed every moment of it.

Diary of a Ready Woman

THE READY WOMAN 💞

After six years of my RN licenses reinstatement, God opened a door that no man could close, and I got my first job as the new Syrita the RN. Won't He, do it? Yes.

I enjoy helping other women recover from the disease of alcoholism through the 12 steps of Alcoholics Anonymous. I am in the process of creating transitional housing for women after rehab treatment.
I continue to take the rejection of "no's" due to my felony record to fuel my purpose and a new passion in life. No longer am I bound by chains.

God has forgiven me, Mr. Golden has forgiven me, and I learned to forgive myself for there is an abundance of FORGIVE-NESS, from our Father. I now live where I remember the forgiveness every day. I live in a church building, and I guess you could say, I reside spiritually and physically IN MY FATHER'S HOUSE.

About the Author

Syrita M. Lindsey MBA, BSN, RN is a native of Columbus, Ohio. She completed her undergraduate studies at Otterbein University. Syrita is a Service Servant for her community as a Registered Nurse. She has worked in various capacities as a nurse in both private and public sectors. Nursing is her passion. She received her Master of Business Administration from the DeVry University. Currently studying to be a Legal Nurse Consultant at Capital University.

Syrita enjoys reading and hiking. Syrita's ongoing mission is providing women who suffer from alcoholism a self-instructed pathway to her recovery.

Slindsay326@gmail.com

www.facebook.com/syrita.lindsey

Dedication and Acknowledgements

To my mother, who gently washed the mud from my body and made me stand once more. Dad, your strength is unparalleled. My family for the relentless prayers and blessing bestowed upon me. Best friend on this side of heaven, Tyrone, for continuously supporting and encouraging my steps with total disregard of my madness. Your friendship has forever changed my attitude towards life. Besties until the end.

Special thanks to Nancie, for the hope and faith shared between two beings in which you are the angel. You are a shooting star seen rarely in one's lifetime. You fought for me when I had no fight left in me. I am forever grateful.

Thank you, readers for allowing me to share my journey may you find hope, courage, and strength within these words.

Personal Notes:

_____

_____

_____

_____

_____

_____

_____

_____

_____

_____

_____

_____

_____

Diary Entry 10

Broken Pieces in a Strong Frame
By Sharonda Grandberry

dear diary

It's me Sharonda...   *June 4, 1994*

Innocence Taken

It was a hot summer day. The humidity was so thick you could hardly breathe. I asked my grandmother if we could go swimming; she said, "yes." I was responsible for ensuring my sister, brother, and cousin arrived at the pool safely. Wiregrass Recreation pool was the place where everyone hangs out, especially the cute boys.

I was 14 years old and in search of the closest feeling of love I could find. I saw some boys from my grandmother's neighborhood and thought it would be cool to chat with them. So we chatted. Then one of the older boys suggested we ride to the store.

I didn't want to seem uncool or anything, so I told my cousin I would be right back and to take care of my sister and brother until I returned. We proceeded to drive to the store, but then the driver took a detour, saying:

"We're going cruising instead."

I agreed to travel if it wasn't going to be long because I had to get back to my cousin and siblings. The passenger reached under the seat and pulled out a brown bag with 80 proof alcohol in it. The cute boy in the back dared me to take a drink. I thought, why not, if it will impress him. I will never forget the taste; it was the worst taste I ever had. They chanted as I drank. We kept riding until we reached a house—the house where I'd lose my innocence forever.

My Father Is Gone

My father committed suicide when I was five years old. I remember his funeral like it was yesterday afternoon. We arrived at the cemetery on a calm sunny day. A gentle breeze filled the air, but sadness lingered all around me. I sat in a chair next to my mother near the burial site and held her hand as she cried profusely. All the family members surrounded his burial site waiting to say their last goodbyes as the casket lowered into the ground.

Suddenly, I heard a loud scream as if someone had murdered something deep within; I saw my mother was slumped over as they lowered my father's body into the ground. The air was filled with silence as they covered his casket. This would be the first broken piece of many to come in my life.

After my father's death, my mother's emotional and mental state was questionable, but who in their right mind would dare question a single black female from the south on how she should raise her children. In elementary school, I reported my mother to my teacher for physical abuse. There was no proof of the bruises on my body because my skin was so dark. The bruises and marks went undetected. The teacher spoke with my mother, and she received a warning. When I returned home that evening, my mother was waiting for me.

She stated: *"If you ever report me to anyone else, I will kill you. I'm your mother. I'm the one who puts clothes on your back and feeds you."* I vowed that day to never tell anyone about the events that occurred in my home. Although my mother took care of me by providing shelter, food, and clothing, she couldn't provide the one thing I longed for most: Unconditional love.

The emotional and physical abuse were unbearable at times. By the age of eight, my mother would slap me so much that I'd sit in the car as we rode in the vehicle with my face against the car window in fear of her hitting me for no reason, which would happen on numerous occasions. I was terrified. I figured out my mother would have flashbacks of the things that transpired in her life during those episodes. My mom would frequently state:

"Your father only married me because I was pregnant with you."

There's an adage that says, "Hurt people hurt people," and this saying proves to be true in my life. My mother was broken herself. She revealed to me that her pregnancy was no fairy tale or a dream come true, but rather I was a mistake. I was the result of a one-night stand. My father and mother had sexual relations for the first time, and she became pregnant.

My mother didn't receive an unforgettable proposal, frequent date nights, or an enormous fancy wedding. She received me. Was I a blessing or a curse? My grandmother didn't believe in premarital sex, so naturally, she expected my father to take care of his responsibility. My father and mother joined hands in holy matrimony, in their attempt to "do the right thing" in the eyesight of God and man. Was it the right thing to do? I know several people that marry in the name of "doing the right thing." I've seen both beauty and chaos in making this kind of decision. My mother was 22, and my father was 21 when they were married. Their marriage lasted three years before the divorce filing.

Emotionally Damaged

During their marriage, my mother stated she experienced physical abuse, emotional abuse, and verbal abuse. My mother's broken pieces came because of a wedding that should have never happened.

Emotionally damaged people, tend to knowingly and unknowingly inflict hurt and pain on other people. For example, a significant percentage of those who have been abused in some form become the abusers of others; those who suffered under an alcoholic parent often themselves will cause their future family to suffer because of their drunkenness.

After my parents' marriage and father's death, the words "Your father only married me because I was pregnant with you" became louder and louder in my ear. The verbal abuse grew, being called names like ugly, smutty, blackie, darkie or fatty, was the norm. I never saw myself as beautiful. I often wondered how anything beautiful could suffer so much ugliness. Was the mistreatment my fault? I was only a child. Broken people often transfer their inner anger onto their family and close friends. I believe my mother's brokenness projected onto myself and at times my siblings.

My sister was born weighing 2lbs. 10 oz., mysteriously none of my mom's children weighed over 3lbs 15oz. My sister had to be in the NICU (Neonatal Intensive Care Unit) for an extended amount of time, which left her learning capability handicapped. My sister appears normal like anyone else, but she is far from normal. My mom would repeatedly call my sister retarded when we were growing up. I found myself doing the same thing on occasions when I'd get mad at my sister, Lashonda if you are reading this, I apologize for every word that caused you pain. My brother had a different father, and anytime my mother would get mad at my brother she'd say:

"You're going to be just like your no-good dad, with his crack-head (user of crack cocaine) self."

My mother showed little to no emotion towards her children. I could never understand why because my grandmother was very affectionate. She would hug and kiss her grandchildren all the time. I longed for my mother's comforting arms to embrace me. My mother reciprocated her love in the form of "buying" more stuff. Finances weren't an issue. My mother, sister and I received a social security check from my father's wages. My brother's father took good care of him, and my mom was a hard worker, so financially we lacked nothing.

I would have preferred the mother and daughter conversations over the new jacket, shoes, or dress. We weren't taught about the Birds and the Bee's, the opposite sex, or the natural process of a woman.

I learned these things on my own. I remember my first encounter with (Auntie Flow) or what's known as the menstrual cycle. I was 12 years old.

I can laugh about the incident now, but at the time it wasn't funny. I was getting ready to go over to my grandmother's house for the day, I ran my bath water to take a bath while sitting on the edge of the bathtub I moved in a certain direction, and that's when it happened. I thought I'd cut myself on the tub as I moved. I was so scared, and I had no idea what was going on. I screamed and called for my mom, she proceeded to laugh and tell me to calm down.

"It's only your period girl." I was relieved but had tons of questions. Questions that I never got answers to.

The Religious Takeover

We did experience happy times mainly during birthdays, holidays, and trips to Panama City Beach, Florida. Christmas was my favorite. The smell of cookies, cakes, and my grandmother's cornbread dressing was a real delight. My mother would always ensure that my siblings and I would have the best Christmas. I always looked forward to the joys of holiday cheer. Christmas stockings, oranges, apples, and peppermint were my favorite. Christmas always brought laughter, then suddenly one day it was gone.

My mother remarried, and we moved from Alabama to Georgia when I was 13. My stepfather was indeed a man of religion. My siblings and I went from a simple religious structure to a religion so strict, that even Jesus would probably have questions. My sister and I weren't allowed to wear pants, attend sports, or school activities, and this was the beginning of the transition.

The transition was tough. I didn't understand why my siblings and I couldn't participate in certain activities anymore, especially Christmas, the only time where I'd experience a worry-free life.

Birthday celebrations ceased to exist as well. We didn't have birthday parties anymore, no skating rink, water parks, at home celebrations, sleepovers, nothing. My mother would attempt to celebrate without my step-father knowing by purchasing us a small gift and our favorite food item during our birthday.

We were on religious lockdown. We could not wear jewelry, eat fast food, drink Kool-Aid, watch cable, nor listen to R&B or soul music. We wore long skirts and dresses and had no FUN! The church became our fun. I was so confused about what do with my new life.

My stepfather made extensive efforts to ensure we'd experience no external influences. He got rid of our music, magazines, and anything that resembled the ways of "the worldly sinners." I was smart, or at least I thought so at the time. I stashed some old cassette tapes for later usage. I would place tissue on the edges of the cassette tapes and record over them with songs from the radio station on the boom box I received during a previous Christmas. I was determined to live somewhat of a normal life.

My stepfather came home early one afternoon while my sister and I were jamming to those cassette tapes. We didn't hear him when he arrived because the music was too loud. He opened the room door and said;

"Turn it off now!"

He confiscated the tapes and the pink and white caboodle I used to hide the tapes. He told my mother what happened and that he would be taking this in the front of the church tonight, her response "Ain't nothing I can do." We arrived at the church, and my heart was beating extremely fast because I knew what was going to happen. My stepfather stood in front of the entire church with my pink and white caboodle and announced to the congregation,

"You need to check your kids' stuff, this is what I found in my child's belongings, Toni Terry, Baby Face, and Hi-Five."

(He didn't know those tapes contained other artists like Ghost Town Dj's, Uncle Luke and the 69 Boyz.) Regardless, I was so embarrassed and publicly humiliated, what a way to start a relationship with my stepfather. Life seemed to get somewhat better, my mother "found the Lord," she didn't curse anymore, and the name calling stopped because it would have been out of her Christian character. We got to visit our grandmother's during the summer break. I love visiting my grandmother because we could finally breathe a little and the religious jail cell would be opened.

I Thought the Worst Was Over

The first channel I would turn to watch was B.E.T for the music videos then I'd ask my grandmother to make a pitcher of Kool-Aid and it seemed as if life was finally looking up, so I thought, until the summer I lost my innocence forever.

It was a hot summer day. The humidity was so thick you could hardly breathe. I asked my grandmother if we could go swimming; she said, "Yes." I was responsible for ensuring my sister, brother, and cousin arrived at the pool safely. Wiregrass Recreation pool was the place where everyone hangs out, especially the cute boys. I was 14 years old and in search of the closest feeling of love I could find. I saw some boys from my grandmother's neighborhood and thought it would be cool to chat with them. We went for a ride, to the house where I'd lose my innocence forever.

Forced into the house with the boys against my will, I tried to scream, but no one could hear me or help me. I remember one of the boys forcing his genitals into my face, and I tried to bite him.

"She tried to bite my dick off; take her into the room," he said.

The effects of the alcohol were starting to kick in, and my fight grew weaker and weaker. My scream grew faint; thrown onto a mattress, the first one climbed on top of me. I begged him to stop but he proceeded to put his condom on as if he didn't hear me at all.

He got done and the second one came in and did the same thing, as did the third one. The fourth and final one didn't even try to put a condom on; he just did his business and got up. I knew three of the guys—we grew up together—but the fourth one I never saw in my life. I cried until I passed out.

In the Fetal Position

I woke up in the car with those boys at my grandmother's driveway. "It's time for you to get out," one boy yelled. It was extremely late; my grandmother was screaming and fussing, but because I was so numb from what had just happened I couldn't hear her. I walked in wearing a white T-shirt. I had no idea where my clothes were. I didn't have any underwear on because they stripped it off. I went into my grandmother's den, locked the door and balled up in a fetal position crying on the cement stairs leading to the room. My grandmother came to the door,

"Sharonda what is wrong with you? I am going to tell your mother." "Grandma, please don't; I will come out in a minute," I replied.

I came out, and my grandmother was distraught with me for leaving my siblings and cousin at the pool. She had no idea what had just transpired.

I Was Fed Up

A week went by. I couldn't eat much. I thought I was going to lose my mind. I called my friend and told her what had happened, and she replied "You need to tell your mom." My friend had no idea of the relationship between my mother and me. I attempted to contact the rape crisis center, but hung up during the process. I was terrified. I ended up taking the advice of my friend: I told my mother.

"You should not have been so fast in the tail (meaning I got what I deserved because I got into the car with those boys). Maybe it would not have happened." Her response left me empty.

I vowed never to tell anyone anything else. I didn't care how much pain I suffered, heartaches I felt, and let-downs I endured. No one would ever know if I was suffering.

The end of my junior year in High school would be the turning point of my life. I had just come from work at the local pizza and sub shop. My mother and I got into a heated disagreement. We were arguing about me going to a high school party at the gym not too far from our house. My mother wasn't allowing me to attend the party. I was determined to participate in the party.

My mom was about to whoop me when I ran to the kitchen grab a knife and drew it out on her. I wanted her to move. I never had any intentions of harming my mother. She was in my way. I was fed up. I was going to the party! She moved out of my way, and I went to the party. I returned home later that night. The locks of our house changed, and my clothes thrown onto the front lawn, I had nowhere to go.

I ended up staying with my boyfriend over the weekend. I had to figure out where I was going to live. Fortunately, my play cousin invited me into her home to live with her until I graduated school and joined the Army. She was a Godsend.

I Never Quit

To survive without living isn't survival at all but to survive and live again shows a resilience that's undeniably a mystery of our faith. If I had to title my life, it would be titled *"Broken Pieces in A Strong Frame."* I've finally arrived at a point in my life where I fully understand that we are not the result of circumstances we go through in life but the strength used to get through those conditions is what defines WHO we are. During the difficult stages of my life, I never QUIT! I now know that God was with me during each episode, incident, situation, and circumstance.

Deuteronomy 31:6 states, "Be strong and courageous. Do not be afraid or terrified because of them, for the LORD your God goes with you; He will never leave you nor forsake you." I relied heavily on prayer during difficult times even as a child. I used to feel sorry for myself and thought my life didn't have a purpose. I contemplated suicide on several occasions because I wanted the pain to end, but there was a RESILIENCE on the inside of me that wouldn't allow me to let go. I didn't understand why I had to go through so much during my childhood. My mother confided in me after I became an adult that her anger was a direct result of the love and attention my father gave me while he was alive.

Jealousy Resided

Her exact words were,

"I was jealous of the relationship you and your dad had. He seemed to show more love and affection towards you then he did me. When I found out you were the only reason he married me, I was devastated. I would have never married your father."

My mother also told me she never received the love and affection she desired from her mother.

"Your grandmother is different with you then she was with me."

My mother was broken like me her frame shattered into many pieces. I've forgiven my mother, and we've reconciled all our differences. I had first to reconcile and forgive myself. Forgiveness was the act. Reconciliation is the process. I had to realize the events that occurred in my life were NOT MY FAULT. The day I lost my innocence WAS NOT MY FAULT. Forgiving those that hurt me, freed me. I broke the curse and could unconditionally love my children. My daughters and I are the best of friends. I couldn't imagine life without any of my kids.

THE READY WOMAN

Today, I am free! I want to help others find their inner keys of freedom and ultimately unlock the beauty that lies within them. I believe that everybody has a story to tell and each story has a different outcome. I desire to travel around the world inspiring others to be the best at being themselves no matter what obstacles they've had to overcome. My motto is: "Love the Skin You're In," meaning regardless of your ethnicity, skin flaws, or imperfect body you should love being YOU because no one else can be a better you!

You may have been broken pieces in a strong frame too but if you don't give up you'll become a beautiful masterpiece in a painting.

About the Author

Plus size Model, Mentor, and Inspirational speaker. Sharonda Grandberry currently resides in Madison Alabama. She is a wife, mother, and friend to many. Sharonda has a dual bachelor's degree in Management and Logistics. Currently employed with the Army Corps of Engineers as a Government Contracts

Specialist. She is an Army veteran who firmly believes in the acronym LDRSHIP, short for Loyalty, Duty, Respect, Service, Honor, Integrity, and Personal Courage. Suicide prevention, selflove, and, personal growth of others through education and resources is what Sharonda strongly believes in.

Sharonda is presently a member/treasurer of Your Heart's Desire Women's Group. An organization that links women with essential community resources while strengthening, encouraging and empowering them through life's transitions.

Sharonda has walked the runway in Full Figured Fierce for CEO Dionne Reeves, designers Tinita LadyLinka Coulter, Chastity Alford owner of The Classic Maven Boutique, and Shelia Lee Designs of Huntsville Alabama. She has also had the privilege of walking for Nashville's O'More School of Design, Lane Bryant, Simply Ke'Shay Boutique in Jacksonville Florida. Sharonda has graced the runway for numerous local designers and boutiques. She has modeled in Havana Cuba as a Brand Ambassador/Model for Classic Maven Boutique located in Jacksonville Florida.

Sharonda is a published fashion stylist in Queen size magazine, and as a plus-size model in FemmePlus and Woman of More Magazine. October 2016, Sharonda was also announced as the winner in the Curvy and Fabulous model of the month on all social media sites belonging to Cynthia Bailey, star of Real Housewives of Atlanta.

Sharonda was named "Miss Alabama Black Expo 2017.

Sharonda has overcome tremendous amounts of adversity to get to the point of where she is now, and that is, she loves the skin she is in! She is currently writing a book titled "Broken Pieces on a Strong Frame" to depict the fight of her life.

sharondagrandberry@gmail.com
www.facebook.com/sharonda.grandberry
www.instagram.com/foreverfashion24_8/

Dedication and Acknowledgements

I'd like to thank my husband, Robert, for his love and support over the years. You are my biggest fan! To my children, Aaliyah, Rodrick, Taikashis, Tykeria, & Nehemiah, you are the reason I push so hard, I always want to be your example.

To my mother, you've taught me the true meaning of forgiveness, patience, and unconditional love. To my siblings, I find strength in your journey. I love you dearly.

To my family near and far, I love you! To my close friends, without your love, support, and encouraging words I don't know how I would have made it over the years. You hold a special place in my heart!

I would like to dedicate my portion of the book to all the people that are/were broken but somehow found the strength to remain active during all of the life's trials. You decided to keep pushing past your brokenness with the power of God and remained steadfast. YOU DID NOT QUIT!

Personal Notes:

_____

_____

_____

_____

_____

_____

_____

Diary Entry 11
May I Have Your Attention
By Dr. Carla Lindsay

dear diary

It's me Carla...   *November 18, 1985*

Daddy's Girl

Rushed to the hospital by my friends, I had taken my college roommate's pills, and nobody knew how many. I was drunk and mad because the guy I liked didn't want anything serious with me. It made me feel invisible. Let's just say, being rushed to the hospital was only the beginning of looking for love in all the wrong places.

I was a Daddy's girl, groomed to feel good whenever I received my Dad's approval. Whether it was making good grades, saving him cookies I baked, or leaving him love notes, I found great value and reward for making my Dad happy.

My father and I had a great relationship. I thought I was his favorite (although we all probably felt that way). He was present in our lives. He came to football games and basketball games to see me cheer. Daddy went to the school to speak to teachers if I made a bad grade we thought I shouldn't have made. We weren't rich, but he always made a way to get me the things I wanted. I remember when Calvin Klein jeans were the craze back in the 80's, I asked for a pair, and he bought them for me. My Dad wasn't perfect (by far), but I knew he loved me and cherished me.

He was the head of his household. The king of his castle. A dominant personality type. I had the kind of Dad that was feared and respected. Growing up, I always told him how I felt. I didn't hold anything back. When I became a teen and older, I held back more and more. When I was younger, I didn't know any better.

189

As I look back, I see how my relationship with my Dad has shaped my relationships with men. I am attracted to what I perceive as power. Whether you were the star football player, the business owner, or the professor, I liked men in the spotlight or power positions. There's nothing wrong with that per se, but a lot comes along with the type of men I found myself going after. The ones I dated and liked were typically not faithful to their women. Since they were in the limelight, every woman around them appeared to want them in the worst way. They have many options. These men are typically dominant personalities. How else would they have gotten the status they have achieved?

I Had to Have Him

I just had to have the star basketball player in high school even though I recognized a classmate of mine was dating him. She had talked about him since we were in middle school. I didn't care they were in a relationship. I saw what I wanted, and I went after him. He dated both of us off and on and others in between. I remember our long talks on the phone, our times at the teen dances, and our secret rendezvous. What I don't remember was being in a real relationship with him.

It seemed like we were always sneaking around. Never proud to be with one another in public. At least, I always thought that was the way he felt. He was my first relationship experience. My future experiences would be built from this relationship lens. Knowing he's seeing other people, that was normal. Sneaking around so that I was the secret, that was normal. Never feeling he was all mine, that was normal.

This relationship I found myself in was the initiation of failed dating experiences for me. I was choosing the wrong men and headed on the path of destructive relationships. When I say destructive, I don't mean physical abuse or mental abuse. But devastating as in this isn't the right type of man for me. This man doesn't belong to me. This man doesn't have my best interest at heart.

When I went to college, it was pretty much the same. I chose someone who only wanted to play. I fell in love. We were never in a committed relationship. He never called me his girl. He never valued me. I was just someone he called over for booty calls. How did I find myself in this same position? In love with someone who was just playing with me. I remember going out to a fraternity party one weekend. I thought we were going to be there together, but he wasn't having it. He acted like I didn't exist. I got drunk, went to my dorm room, and took a bunch of my roommate's pills. I never thought I wanted to kill myself; I guess I just wanted the attention.

My friends rushed me to the hospital, and they called him. He came to see me, but nothing changed. I realized he wasn't a bad person. He just wasn't ready to settle down and be seriously committed to me. He started bringing another woman around, and so that was it for us.

I didn't date much in grad school. I studied and partied and studied some morE. A relationship wasn't the priority at that time. I just wanted to finish school, leave Memphis, and get back home to Kentucky. Being around mostly Caucasians didn't help any. Not that I wouldn't date outside my race, but I really wasn't interested in many of the guys there.

I remember getting friendly with one of the guys in the class ahead of me. We would speak on the phone and talk when we saw each other in school. One night he called and asked if he could come over. By that time, I was comfortable with him, so I said ok. When he got there, I opened the door, walking in, he said:

"I brought a friend with me."

I was a little surprised, but I knew his friend, so I let them in. Of course, they had no right intentions towards me. They wanted to have a threesome! I was not having any of that so I kicked them out. I know that situation could have turned out very differently. I saw that guy years later at a conference, and I could tell he was feeling a little awkward.

His Name Was Brad

Graduate school was uneventful. I moved to Nebraska with a friend just to get my head right and get ready for the real world after so many years of being a student. I got a job at the local optical shop. I thought it was going to be business as usual, but the experience changed my life. I met someone his name was Brad, and we worked together. We started out as co-workers, and I tried to fix him up with my roommate. We became friends, we went out after work along with other coworkers, and we enjoyed each other's company. We both wanted to go to an amusement park in Kansas City, so we planned a trip to go.

We had a great time, but since the drive was three hours, we decided to get a hotel room. We got one room with two beds. We started out in separate beds but ended up in the same bed. We didn't have sex. We just talked, kissed, and cuddled. That was the beginning of a great relationship.

We were inseparable. Everyone at work figured out we were dating, so it became common knowledge that we were together. It felt good to be in a real relationship where both people cared for one another and respected each other. I had never experienced that before. And by the way, Brad was Caucasian. Our race was never an issue for us. I remember one evening the employees and one past employee (Amy) went out to celebrate the manager's birthday. We were eating, drinking and talking around the table, and Amy says,

"Brad, are you dating anybody?"

"Actually, Carla and I are dating."

"No way."

"Brad nodded his head and said: "Yes, we're in a relationship."

That was music to my ears! No one had ever said that. No one had ever 'claimed' me as their girl.

Another time Brad showed me he was a great guy, had to do with his ex. We were at work one evening, and he got a call on his cell. He came to me and told me it was Sarah. She was in the area and wanted to come by with her daughter to see him. He told her no. It wouldn't be appropriate because he was dating someone, and it wouldn't be right for her daughter. He was a real stand-up guy. Brad and I dated for about six months, and then I moved to Atlanta to start my career. We had a good relationship, but I knew he wasn't my life partner. It was hard leaving Nebraska, but I knew I was only there temporarily. We kept in touch for a few months, but we eventually grew apart.

The Church Girl

Life in Atlanta was everything I thought it would be except I was still single. My career was on course, I bought a new car, and I purchased a house. Something was missing. I had a longing that I never felt before. I didn't grow up in church, but I knew about Christianity because my Mom went to church. So, I thought I should start going.

I visited a few churches and ended up giving my life to Christ at Ben Hill UMC. That was it! The missing piece, the longing. It was a personal relationship with Christ. When I became saved, I gave my all to Him. I was in church every Sunday, I took every class I could to learn more, I studied the Bible consistently, and I started living a celibate lifestyle.

Life was good! I was still single, but I knew God had someone for me. Through my studies and church, I learned that I was valuable. I learned that I was a gift. God loved me no matter what. I read the Bible from cover to cover, and I believed what it said.

I soon met someone else, Keith. He was very nice looking, and we worked together. It took a while for me to take his advances seriously, but I finally did. He knew up front that I was celibate. We went on a few dates and then decided to become monogamous.

I never believed that Keith was the one for me, but I went forward with the relationship anyway. I liked him, but it wasn't love. We dated for about eight months, but my uncertainty about us got to him. I understood. I couldn't even tell him 'I love you' because I didn't feel that way about him.

The relationship with Keith made me realize that I needed to date more to get married. I'm not talking about dating just to be with someone, that always ends up with somebody getting hurt. But if you know from the beginning this person isn't who you want to marry then don't date them. This way of dating can be lonely, but you will be happier in the long run.

He Would Never

The last relationship I was in, I met him at church. He was attractive, he was a business owner, and he was a Christian. I thought he was the one. My naiveté' of relationships blinded me. Gary had two children (I thought) and he was divorced. After about three months of dating, he wanted to be exclusive. I was in la-la land. Happy to be in a relationship and happy to finally be with someone who could be the one.

I remember having dinner with a friend and telling her that Gary would never cheat on me. He was family oriented and he loved me. She said I hear what you're saying but be careful because a man will be a man. Well, he was cheating. I was devastated. I never saw it coming. I didn't pay attention to the red flags. I practically begged him to take me back, to choose me.

We ended up getting back together, but it was different for me. I was jaded. I didn't trust him anymore. A relationship couldn't survive in that environment. A few months later he was at it again. Always coming up with an excuse why he was doing what he was doing. You're a doctor, I own a plumbing business, he would say. You're too good for me, you're a professional. I'm just a blue-collar worker. Ahh, so that was it.

He never felt he was good enough for me, so he cheated on me before I cheated on him (so he thought). Of course, with that type of thinking, a relationship would go nowhere. Gary and I dated off and on for a couple of years until I realized I deserved better. Not better in the sense of someone with a better job, but better in that I deserved someone who treated me like a queen.

After the breakup with Gary, I went to seminary. I obtained a master's degree in Christian counseling. Throughout my studies, I learned a lot about men and relationships. I learned that if I didn't value me, then no one else would appreciate me. I learned to be at peace with my singleness knowing that my Daddy (God) had some-one for me. I took relationship classes every chance I got.

I became certified in giving the Prepare/Enrich assessment for engaged and married couples which allowed me to get up close and personal with couples. I put together the premarital program at my church in which they still use today. I am a certified life coach and dating/relationship, coach. I have always loved love! I love see-ing people in thriving relationships. I'm finally at my best self men-tally and I'm ready to experience the type of relationship I coach my clients to prepare for.

THE READY WOMAN

How do you go from having low self-esteem and being in one bad relationship after another to knowing your value and worth and waiting for the relationship God has for you? Well for me, it took lots of doing things the wrong way and finding out that wasn't right for me. And then deciding I wanted more. I wanted to be happy and in a Godly relationship.

I knew I wanted my life to change so I had to make some deci-sions. I thought moving to Atlanta would be all it took to start fresh, but I was wrong. I moved here, got a job, bought a car, and a new house; but I was still empty.

I had a hole in my heart that only God could fill. I gave my life to Christ, and everything changed. I became spiritually, emotionally, and mentally vibrant. My mindset did a 360. I knew I was fearfully and wonderfully made, and no one could tell me any different. I finally valued myself. I wouldn't take less than God's best for my life. It didn't happen overnight, but it was a process. Giving my life to Christ was the best thing that has ever happened to me. That was my first step to becoming a Ready Woman! I'm not saying you must become a Christian, but you do need a mindset shift. You need to understand that you are more precious than gold. You have worth and value. You deserve the desires of your heart, and you deserve nothing but the best.

Next, I set some goals for my life, long term and short term. I thought about the things I wanted to accomplish in my life and things I wanted to do. I want to travel. I want to pamper myself by getting massages on a regular basis, getting my hair done every week, and trying a new restaurant at least once a month. I wanted to work on getting debt free. I worked on my physical self. I am exercising more and eating better. I'm still a work in progress! I made the decision to be the best me I could be. Accomplishing goals, I set made me happy. I had joy. I was doing the doggone thing. I was living life.

During this time in my life, I didn't date much. I went out here and there, but nothing serious or lasting. I decided I didn't want to date just to be doing something. I only wanted to go out with someone I felt a connection with or someone that interests me. I have always wanted to be married and have a large family. Both of those still elude me today, but I still have joy and I know God has someone for me. Yes, I get discouraged sometimes, but my Daddy (God) has my back. I must keep the faith.

I am living in expectation. The goals I had set, the work I did to get them accomplished, and my belief, all came together to make me expect nothing but the best for myself. Living in expectation means that you don't take no for an answer. It means that nothing is impossible for you.

Whatever God says you can have, you can have it. When you live in that type of expectation, it doesn't bother you that you don't have everything you want because you are always expecting what you are lacking. You should know that it is coming in due time, or if not, something better is on the way.

I am still transforming and going through this process. You find out during trying times that your mindset isn't quite right about something, so then you have to go through the process to fix it. I still have goals I am trying to accomplish. If you are living, there are always new challenges to take on. I have come a long way from that insecure girl that grew up in Kentucky. I am now a Ready Woman. Ready to take on the world and all it has for me!

About the Author

Dr. Carla Lindsay is from Paris, Kentucky but currently resides in Atlanta Georgia. She completed her undergraduate studies at Eastern Kentucky University. After only three years of undergrad, she enrolled at Southern College of Optometry where she received her bachelor's in biology and Doctor of Optometry degrees. Dr. Lindsay has been in Georgia for 21 years and has been practicing for over 20 years. After being in many modes of practice including retail, employed, and private; she opened her practice, Eye Max Vision Care Group (inside Pearle Vision), in 2007.

Her passion for helping others has led her to be active in community service projects with her church and other organizations. She enjoys mission work with the One Sight Organization and has done missions in India, Jamaica, China, Mexico, Liberia, Ghana, Nicaragua, Tanzania, and Haiti. In 2004 Dr. Lindsay received a Master's in Christian Counseling with an emphasis on marriage and relationships.

She has counseled many couples successfully and is currently using her skill and training as a Certified Matchmaker. Dr. Lindsay has a passion for thriving relationships and wants to see and help couples succeed. She started Heart2Heart Introductions in 2015 where she coaches singles to be the best they can be, and she also helps them find the love of their life.

Drcarla@theringisthegoal.com

www.facebook.com/Heart2HeartIntroductions

www.instagram.com/drcarlah2h/

Dedication and Acknowledgement

I want to thank my parents, John Lindsay and Shirley Brack, who are in heaven for instilling in me that I can be anything I want to be when I put my mind to it and do the work that is necessary. I also thank my family and friends for always encouraging me and believing in me.

Personal Notes:

_____

_____

_____

_____

_____

_____

_____

_____

_____

_____

_____

_____

_____

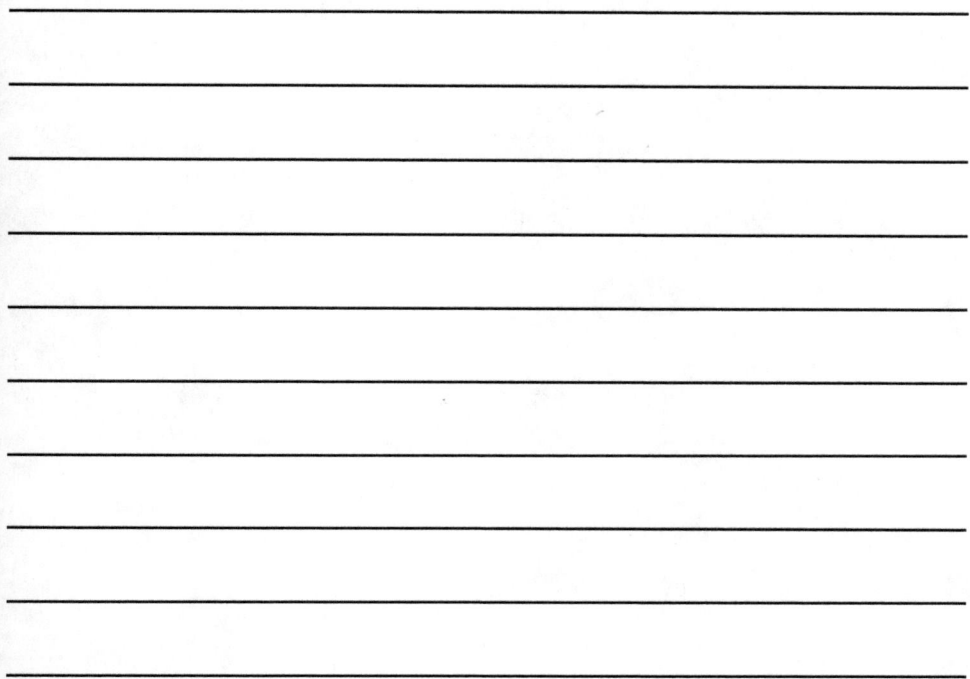

Diary Entry 12
No, Not My Cherry
By LaTonya Spates

dear diary

It's me LaTonya...   *September 16, 1991*

Feeling Paralyzed

I ran to the window and looked out in disbelief. It was gone! The reliable transportation I had for my two children and me. It was my pride! I poured my blood, sweat, and tears into my car. Still, in a tank top and pajama bottoms, I rushed outside to see if it was true. I was greeted by the cold wintery brisk air of a typical January morning in Norfolk VA. My life was a dreadful nightmare because everything I worked so diligently for was gone. My car and my possessions inside.

I was numb, feeling paralyzed. My heart sank into my stomach and I was so confused and directionless. My mind is racing with hundreds of thoughts at one time. My feelings are hurt, and my kids have a dentist appointment the same day, not to mention I still needed to report to work. I felt my car repossession was the straw that broke the camel's back, and I was just given a ten-day notice to be out of my apartment.

Trying to Cope

To cope, I start thinking when times were more comfortable. Well, at least my parents made it seem that way when I was a little girl. My dad was such an intelligent man. He managed to make it out of the impoverished streets of Norfolk Virginia by obtaining his Bachelor of Science in Electrical Engineering and brought his six children all the way to Newport, Rhode Island to experience a better future.

As my mind ventured back in time, I remember Hall Avenue was an excellent place to live. It seemed as if we had it all. We were living the American dream. Dad was an engineer by day and a fisherman by night. Every time I saw that '69 Chevy Cutlass leave the driveway I knew he was on a mission. I guess he had to be gone and work hard to maintain our two-story, four bedrooms with two bathrooms, New England style home. We never seemed to lack a thing.

Friday evenings were full of pizza or Chinese and Dunkin Donuts. On Sunday mornings, sometimes he would take us to the Newport Creamery downtown for an "Awful Awful." The drink didn't get its' name because it was terrible, but because it was big. My dad was always gone it seemed, and sometimes I wondered would he leave to clear his head of the pain of dealing with mom being sick or was it work related?

Mom in and Out of the Hospital

I watched my mom prick herself every day to get her insulin but never really realized exactly how sick she was until I was about six or seven years old. I just always thought that she was tired and just needed rest. She was in and out of the hospital. She masked her pain well. I guess she didn't want us to know how excruciating the pain was. My mother was such a chef at heart. There were many days I woke up to the delicious smell of homemade pancakes. I can still see the savory stuffed green peppers and juicy pickled watermelon peels.

My two sisters Sherry, Veronica, and I would play in the snow for hours. When we were ready to return home, mom greeted us with hot chocolate, homemade cookies, and a movie. Mom was so loving and nurturing.

Tragedy Hits Home Hard

One fateful day things took a turn for the worse. Diabetes became life-threatening. The next couple of months we witnessed our mom go through procedures that seemed to drain the life out of her.

After each dialysis treatment, she always appeared to feel and look so weak. However, how she felt never stopped her from trying to fix my hair with braids and get my siblings and me ready for school.

It was September 15, 1991, a usual day. We visited mom at the hospital. My mom was hospitalized what seemed like permanently now. My dad was missing her like crazy. You can tell that he wasn't used to a life of her not being home with all of us. This visit was so strange because mom was sicker than usual. She kept telling us how much she loved us. She even told me how I needed to look out for my brother Steven. She kept saying,

"You hear me?" I remember because school had just started and not having her home was difficult.

That night the doctors came in her room more than usual checking her vital signs and asking so many questions. Something just didn't sit right with dad. He was walking back and forth pacing the floor anxiously. Then suddenly mom got so sick that they asked us to leave out and maybe come back tomorrow because she needed rest.

Complications from the diabetes were taking a toll on her fragile body each dialysis session. Dad decided that it was time for us to go home for the night. As we kissed her goodbye and proceeded out the door, I caught a glimpse of her weary face as the door was closing. I got such an eerie feeling that still gives me goosebumps till this day. This night I cried and begged my dad to stay longer, but, he insisted that we must get home because we had school in the morning.

It was a beautiful sunny morning on September 16, 1991. I was finished getting ready for school, grabbed my book bag, and was headed out the door when the phone rang. How awkward the phone never really rang these days unless it was the school or hospital.

My dad answered with a *"Hello, yes, this is William Spates, her husband."*

The next thing I heard was a holler I've never heard from any man in my life. It was so blood curling and symbolized deep dark pain. He kept screaming:

"No, not my Cherry," repeatedly and dropped the phone. By the time, he reached me in the hallway, I was already in tears. He told me

"Tonya, momma's gone."

Mom Is Gone, and So Is Dad

The next couple of weeks seemed to move so fast I barely remember it all.   All I know is my dad went plum crazy and had nervous breakdown after nervous breakdown. Dad hospitalized and heavily medicated. My oldest sister Sherry was at the house playing mom because we had no one. My two older brothers Butch and Neil were already out of the house at this point, so we were left to fend for ourselves. We had a couple of cousins on my dad's side come up and try and help, but it did more harm than good. Eventually, Aunt Judy who is my mother's sister who lived in Chesapeake Virginia got word of everything going on. The next thing I know we were being moved from the north to the south and planning my mother's funeral.

That long ride to my aunt's house from Newport to Chesapeake felt like an eternity. It was a ride we had taken so many times before, the difference this time was that my sweet mother wasn't with us. I consider my loving Aunt Judy to be my guardian angel sent to me from heaven above. She took on the ardent task of raising my two sisters Sherry and Veronica, brother Steven, and I. If it weren't for her we would have gone into the foster care system, possibly separated and put up for adoption.

Aunt Judy had a 15-year-old daughter of her own named Dominique and was caring for her bedridden paralyzed father. We didn't have much space, but we made it work. It was a three-bedroom, one bath, brick style single family home with a den that was turned into a bedroom.

Aunt Judy Worked It Out

Aunt Judy never treated us like we were any different from her daughter. She never picked sides when we argued, and she treated us like we were her very own. I don't think her daughter was too thrilled about the transition and it took a lot of getting used too.

Money was scarce at times. Aunt Judy worked two to three jobs just to make ends meet. The $400 she was receiving from the state wasn't sufficient to meet our needs. We went through some tumultuous times sometimes. But with the grace of God, he kept us. I couldn't grace the school halls with the latest name brand fashions. I was often bullied and went home in tears. I felt like I didn't belong and always wished I could take a boat or plane far away. Other kids would ask me where I was from and tell me that I talk funny. I managed to go through school excelling academically at everything I did. I can't begin to tell you how many certificates and honors I received. Somehow and someway I stayed focused. I just had this fire in me to succeed. I felt like I had so much to prove. I was so determined that failing was not an option. I knew that's what my mother would've wanted.

Aunt Judy always encouraged my siblings and me. She wanted us to have better. She, unfortunately, had to drop out of high school to help my grandma. It was difficult seeing my friends with their parents sometimes because it brought sadness to my heart especially during the holidays, birthdays, and special events at school. I was forever longing to have my dad around. He was diagnosed with paranoid schizophrenia so unless he was on his medication we couldn't be around him. You could tell he wanted to be able to raise us, but due to his illness, he was found mentally incapable.

Daddy's Back

Around the end of what seemed to be my middle to high school years, my dad was well enough to come around. I mean he came around before sometimes but it always seemed so short lived because he would still wind up in a hospital again or residential living facility.

It's like the doctors had finally come up with the perfect concoction to keep him grounded. He was their guinea pig, and now I know why it's called a medical practice. The doctors used my daddy and his condition for practice.

Those were exceptional years because I felt I had my father back. He would take all my friend and me to the beach. He even taught me how to drive when I was 16. Little did I know that those years would be short-lived.

A few years later he was hospitalized and put in an assisted living facility where he had more supervision. When I was 19-years-old, I started handling my father's affairs because the living facility he was living in was mistreating him and taking his money. It was so hard to see my father suffer that way.

Most of my friends were just about almost ready to enter the workforce with their degrees when I decided to go back to school for business administration at the age of 21. I felt so far behind. But I couldn't be mad at anyone but myself. I am the one who decided I needed a break before going to college that turned into three years.

Together Again

In 2004 at the age of 23, I took it upon myself with a prayer to God above to move out of my aunt's home, so I could adequately care for my father. Once again, he was poorly cared for at an assistant living facility. I moved to Huntersville with my Dad, Veronica, her two children, and Steven. It felt like we were together again! With the new-found responsibility of rent of my new house, I was forced to work full-time instead of part-time as before. Working full-time frustrated my ability to go to college and I put my education on the backburner.

I worked odd jobs for three to four years. One position I didn't care for but I made the most money there was selling directories. . It sometimes required outbound calling. I couldn't stand the idea of taking away from someone's dinner with a silly phone call and getting cussed out. I managed to remain there for almost five years.

Through the Fire

Somewhere in the middle of those years, March of 2005, my world felt like it came crashing down. It was a pretty, sunny, and windy day. I was taking calls on the phone in the middle of the day, and my phone just wouldn't stop ringing. Veronica was calling me. But why I thought? Can't it wait? I figured I would just call her later. The phone rang again, again, and again. Something just wasn't right. I asked the caller to hold and then proceeded to my manager's desk. I told him I think there is an emergency.

He told me to go into the hallway to take the call. I answered the phone to a very frantic and overwhelmed Veronica. She shouted that I had to come quick. She told me that our house was on fire. What? I was thinking. I grabbed my keys and ran. I was moving so fast I don't even remember getting in the car. I recalled going about 80 mph on the highway and kept thinking if I get pulled over the cops would understand.

The next couple of miles felt like it took forever before I reached my street. The 1500 block of Dungee Street looked like the scene from an action movie. The firefighters or police wouldn't let me come down the road. I yelled to them that I lived there, but it seemed they didn't even care. They kept asking us to move. I just wanted to know where my family was. I parked my car in the middle of the road and hopped out.

I caught a glimpse of my sister at a neighbor's house with her children. She proceeded to tell me that a little boy was playing with a lighter next door to us. He set his grandmother's mattress on fire. The story around the way was that someone tried to drag it down the stairs and put it outside, but the house engulfed in flames. The fire managed to spread to our home and three other neighboring homes as well. The firefighters and police said that if it hadn't been so windy, the fire wouldn't have spread so much. My sister said she was about to take a nap when everything happened.

She wanted to stay awake because Oprah was talking about living your dreams and she didn't want to miss it. As she dozed off, she heard someone banging on the door so hard that it woke her out of her sleep. It was the Norfolk Fire Department. They told her she needed to get out because her house was on fire. Thankfully she left safe with my niece and nephew. My father was at the library and brother at work. Thank goodness everyone was safe!

My brother Steven and I had nothing salvageable from our rooms. Just the thought of everything that I worked so hard for and earned gone, simply brought tears to my eyes... Everything seemed to crumble like paper. The only thing that did survive from my room was my bible. The cover a little charred but none of the pages. How powerful!

Veronica and Dad had items, but there was so much water damage that they weren't any good anymore. I was never more famous in my life than that week. Everyone was saying how they saw me on TV. Every news channel in the area was at my house before I even went in. The kept asking us, "How do you feel?" How would you feel if you lost everything you owned? The news will do anything for a story I tell you. Isn't that adding insult to injury?

Starting Over Again

The saying goes, 'Whatever doesn't kill you makes you stronger.' The next couple of weeks and months required a lot of hard work as we looked for a place to lay our heads. The Red Cross helped us with vouchers for food, clothes, and lodging the first night. They also gave us the hope that when we found a place that they would pay the first month's rent and deposit. My pastor at the time Dr. Jackie Murphy let us stay with her until we could find a place of our own. With the help of so many co-workers, family, and church family, it gave us the courage to move forward. People from my job raised money from a bake sale and donated it to me, along with food, clothes, and personal donations. It was so good to have people who care and that were willing to give at a time of need selflessly.

Rising from the ashes

Deep down inside I knew that I always wanted to have better. I loved doing hair... I had been doing my hair since I was twelve. My cousin Dominique has been doing hair since I could remember. I was always fascinated watching her style and do hair. It was always my passion... I came to a breaking point in 2005. I was able the following year to pursue my dream. My future happiness was at stake. I visited Rudy and Kelly Academy of Hair and Nails (A Paul Mitchell Partner School). It was indeed one of a kind, and I was blown away by the culture. Everything about it was excellent.

The staff was so upbeat and made me believe I could move mountains. I knew this was where I wanted to attend right away. I'm very thankful to Mr. Rudy, Mrs. Karen Beven, Mrs. Joyce, and Mrs. Genie for your love and encouragement. I proceeded to go through enrollment but ran into significant financial difficulty trying to get started. I got approved for a loan, but I needed $325 for books up front before I could start.

Once again, I was sent another angel named Donetta Johnson who is a family friend. All she asked is that I pay it forward. She wrote me a check, and I was able the following year to pursue a lifelong dream of becoming a licensed cosmetologist.

It felt like I was born to do this. I joined every possible team in school and tried to be as much a part of the Paul Mitchell culture as I could be. I loved every minute of it! In the end, I gained my reward. I graduated top of my class in April 2008. On my 27th birthday in May, I took my state board licensing exam for cosmetology. I excelled considerably again and shortly later that month I began working at Bubbles Salon in Lynnhaven Mall.

Trying to establish myself in the industry was difficult with two little ones and little to no support from their father. So yes, the car repossession, homeless shelters and starting repeatedly were all part of the process of realizing my dreams and releasing lack and limitations from my life.

THE READY WOMAN

Sometimes dreams can seem so far away and unattainable, especially when you've had to overcome so much before arriving at your purpose. We have no control over the cards we are dealt in life, but, we do over how we play the game. I am a living, walking, talking, and breathing miracle that anything is possible if you just believe. Never give up and never stop striving no matter the outside appearances. Have faith in God, knowing anything is possible for you.

SUCCESS

Success is a measure of how far you have come.

How much you have achieved and how much you have conquered.

Success is what lies ahead to obtain and what it takes to grasp it.

Success is every dream being fulfilled and manifested.

Success isn't acquired easily.

It is full of mess ups, do-overs, quirks, and headaches.

Every milestone reached is a goal obtained.

Sometimes while trying to achieve success, the road gets bumpy.

Nevertheless, try and exceed with great excellence, and you will see that success is only a heartbeat away.

I am a Ready Woman as a proud mother and one of Norfolk's Best Master Stylist.

ONE LIFE

We have one life to give, to live, to share.

To have love and compassion for those we care for most.

To live life to its very fullest.

In spite of circumstances, problems, and situations.

There is a way of escape and a place of refuge and hope.

Here you can find inner peace and fulfill life's desires.

Put away all hate, envy, and strife and live this one life.

I know you want and need better.

You have aspirations and dreams that need to be achieved. Share what you know, encourage somebody's heart. Come and go with me, let's live this one life.

LaTonya Spates

About the Author

Once a New Englander, always a New Englander. That is the motto. Born and partially raised in Newport, Rhode Island, but moved to Chesapeake, Virginia at the tender age of 10 years old to be raised by her aunt after the death of her mother and mental breakdown of her father. LaTonya has risen from the ashes of a difficult life beginning, and now excels as a master hair stylist and full-figured model living in Norfolk Virginia. She is blessed with two beautiful children, Azaria and Elijah, who are her inspiration.

You may have seen her as a contestant for Cycle 2 of Curvy Idol, The Full-Figured Fierce Face of August 2016, or as a model for Virginia Full Figured Fashion Week, The 4th Annual Heartbeat Gala, and Fifty Shades of Shears Hair and Fashion Show. The face of Queen of the curves September 2017.

lmariespates@gmail.com
www.facebook.com/spatesplusmodeldiva1
www.instagram.com/ladyt_thehairdiva

Dedication and Acknowledgements

I would like to dedicate this book in the loving memory of my parents, William and Cherry Spates. I want to thank my Aunt Judy Penn for the many sacrifices made and love in abundance she showed to build me up after the passing of my mother and father.

Personal Notes:

_____

_____

_____

_____

_____

_____

_____

_____

_____

_____

_____

_____

_____

dear diary .

To You the Reader,

Thank you for sharing our experiences as The Ready Woman Society. If you are interested in being in our upcoming volume of **Diary of a Ready Woman**, please email your contact information and one paragraph sharing your story of allowing your comeback to be better than your setback. We want to hear from you.

Write us at **ReadyWomanPublishing@gmail.com**

Get your copy of **The Ready Woman**, How to Bounce Back from Adversity, Redesign Your Life for Amazing Love & Real Happiness in 9 Steps. **By Nekisha Michelle Kee**

www.readywoman.co

If you are interested in hosting a Diary of a Ready Woman author event & monologues in your city, organization, or church please email your request to **ReadyWomanPublishing@gmail.com**

Please follow and support the co-authors of this book individually on social media and join the online forum where we'll be discussing the book and sharing our upcoming online and live events at:

www.facebook.com/groups/diaryofareadywoman

XOXO,
The Ready Woman Society